With the fine precision of a theologian, the clear perception of a teacher, and the warm affection of a pastor, Robert Strivens walks us quickly but carefully through the landscape of confessional conviction. He plainly sets out the principles of Reformed Baptist faith and life, and pointedly identifies the related practices of righteousness. He has laboured to be clear and simple without being careless or shallow. The result is an accessible volume which will help any Christian, especially those confessional Baptists who wish to know better 'the things most surely believed among us.'

~Jeremy Walker

Pastor of Maidenbower Baptist Church, editor of *Rooted and Grounded: a light modernisation of the 1689 Baptist Confession of Faith*

You have in your hands a lucid and concise exposition of the Second London Baptist Confession of Faith. It will serve as an invaluable primer, an introduction to historic biblical Christianity. Robert Strivens consistently drives home the importance and relevance of these doctrines both for churches and for individual Christians. Here is truth to live by.

~Austin Walker

Retired pastor, author of *The Excellent Benjamin Keach*

The 1689 Handbook

*A chapter-by-chapter introduction to the
Second London Baptist Confession of Faith*

by Robert Strivens

GRACE PUBLICATIONS TRUST
62 Bride Street
London N7 8AZ
www.gracepublications.co.uk

First published in Great Britain by Grace Publications Trust 2025.

A record for this book is available from the British Library.

Cover design by Pete Barnsley (CreativeHoot.com)

Printed in the UK by Ashford Colour Ltd.

ISBN Paperback: 978-1-917322-00-3
       Ebook: 978-1-917322-01-0

The 1689 Handbook

A chapter-by-chapter introduction to the
Second London Baptist Confession of Faith

by Robert Strivens

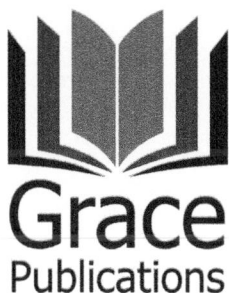

Grace
Publications

*To the members and congregation of
Bradford on Avon Baptist Church (founded 1689).
With heartfelt thanks for your love for Christ
and faithfulness to his word.*

Contents

Foreword

by Professor Michael Haykin

I have long been happy, and honoured, to identify myself with the Particular, or Calvinistic, Baptist community of churches. This tradition of church life has a long and rich history that stretches back to the mid-seventeenth century, but due to its embrace of Reformation truths and Ancient Church confessions, its roots stretch back through the sixteenth century to the earliest centuries of Christian witness. Moreover, I firmly believe that this tradition retains some of the key elements of the ecclesial witness of the New Testament.

This ecclesiological tradition is obviously baptistic as well as congregational – and it is also notably confessional. In English-speaking Baptist life during the nineteenth-century, especially in North America, there emerged the idea that being Baptist has little or nothing to do with confessions. The important freedom of soul liberty – that men and women and children must freely choose to follow Christ – was set over against being confessional, and it was argued that confessions and creeds were unnecessary restrictions of this freedom.

The truth of the matter is quite different. From their specific origins in the seventeenth century, the earliest Particular Baptists believed in the importance of confessions. Witness, in this regard, the First and Second London Baptist Confessions (1644/46 & 1677/89). In fact, the Second London Baptist Confession, popularly known as the 1689 Confession, is undoubtedly the most important confessional text in Particular Baptist history. It helped shape the history of these churches on both sides of the Atlantic throughout the long eighteenth century – even though it was not in print for much of this era. If one looks at the confessional abstracts that were employed by the various local Baptist associations in England during this period of time, for example, the fingerprints of the 1689 Confession are quite evident. And authors like Abraham Booth, Andrew Fuller, and Samuel Pearce cite or allude to this document. This text was critical to the remarkable ministry of C. H. Spurgeon during the last half of the nineteenth century – he had it reprinted early in his ministry in the 1850s – a ministry that continues to be influential in Baptist life even today. And when the school where I teach, The Southern Baptist Theological Seminary, was founded in 1859, Basil Manly, Jr. specifically employed the Second London Confession to craft Southern's confessional foundation, The Abstract of Principles.

Thus, it is with a deep sense of thanks that I commend this fresh commentary on the 1689 Confession by Dr. Robert Strivens. It is a helpful guide to the theological and spiritual riches of this text, presenting not only the original provenance of this text, but also demonstrating its contemporary importance.

Michael A. G. Azad Haykin

Dundas, Ontario, 29th May 2025.

Director of The Andrew Fuller Center for Biblical Studies

and Professor of Church History and Biblical Spirituality at

Southern Baptist Theological Seminary

Preface

Many years ago, a friend advised me to undertake a close study of one of the reformed confessions of faith. This was soon after he and I had completed our seminary studies and were in pastoral ministry. Despite all the advantages of the excellent course that we had pursued, I felt a strong need to study more deeply the historic doctrine of the Christian faith that we were seeking to preach and teach, in order to help me in my pastoral work. My experience of the practicalities of the pastorate convinced me of my own need to be securely rooted in a historic and systematic presentation of biblical truth.

I failed to take my friend's advice. I foolishly allowed the daily pressure of ministry to squeeze out the time that I could have given to such study. I deeply regret that it was not until much later in my ministry that I came to engage closely with the reformed confessions – especially the one formulated by the reformed Baptists of the later part of the seventeenth century: the 1677/89

Second London Baptist Confession of Faith (or the '1689 Confession', as I shall mostly refer to it in this book, for the sake of brevity).

My study of the 1689 Confession and of other reformed confessions of faith has convinced me of the need in our day to recover a greater familiarity with these historic statements of orthodox Christian doctrine. Such a recovery would be of inestimable benefit to individual Christian believers, but also – and especially – to churches which put the time and effort needed into digging into the great truths which these confessions express.

These are truths to live by – not merely to understand intellectually, but to believe in the heart and live out in daily service to Christ. They will shape us as individual believers, but most importantly they will also shape the life of our churches. Christian life is nothing if it is not lived out in fellowship with Christian brothers and sisters in the local church and the 1689 Confession is of the greatest help to that end. The reason for this is simple – that the Confession expresses succinctly and clearly the great doctrines of the Bible.

I owe much to many people who have helped and encouraged me in the preparation of this book. The book originated as a series of articles in *Reformation Today*, the magazine of Reformation Today Trust which exists to promote reformed Baptist teaching and practice and whose theological basis is the 1689 Confession. I am grateful to the trustees for permission to reproduce the articles, in a somewhat revised form, in this volume. I am also especially grateful to Oliver Allmand-Smith, Bill James, Mostyn Roberts, Rob Ventura, Austin Walker and Jeremy Walker for their thoughts and comments on draft chapters. My thanks too to Helen Gray for her meticulous and always gracious editing of the manuscript and to

Andrew Roycroft for his wisdom, advice and enthusiasm in guiding the book to its final form and into the market place. As ever, the love, patience and support of my wife Sarah has been of incalculable benefit.

Robert Strivens
Bradford on Avon
30th September 2024

Where can I find the 1689 Confession of Faith?

The original text of the Confession can be found online as well as in a variety of published sources, including William L. Lumpkin, *Baptist Confessions of Faith*, 2nd edn., rev. Bill J. Leonard (King of Prussia, PA: Judson Press, 2011). A facsimile of the 1677 Confession has been published by B&R Press.

Modernised versions of the Confession have been produced: most recently, Jeremy Walker, ed., *Rooted & Grounded: A Light Modernisation of the 1689 Baptist Confession of Faith* (Leyland: EP Books, 2021).

Introduction:
Why the 1689 Confession?

The 1689 Confession of Faith – more fully, the 1677/1689 Second London Baptist Confession of Faith – is the main confession of faith of reformed Baptists. It represents the full flowering of the movement to formulate confessions of faith among reformed churches in the sixteenth and seventeenth centuries.

The 1689 Confession was largely neglected over the course of the last century, but the new millennium has seen a welcome revival of interest in this remarkable work of the early particular – that is, reformed or calvinistic – Baptists. Though it originated in England, the Confession has international reach: it formed the basis in America for the Philadelphia Confession of 1742; Joshua Thomas translated the Confession into Welsh in 1792 and the Confession is now available in many different languages across the world.

This book seeks to introduce to the reader the riches of the 1689 Confession and show how its teaching benefits individuals and churches in the twenty-first century. It works through the thirty-two chapters of the Confession consecutively, often grouping chapters on a theme together. To start, we must introduce the Confession itself.

History

The 1689 Confession of Faith does not date from the year 1689. It was first printed in 1677. Its origin probably lies in the Particular Baptist congregation which met in Petty France, London. The document is seemingly the work of the two ministers of that congregation at the time, Nehemiah Coxe and William Collins.

In 1677, Charles II was on the throne of England and laws were in place which imposed severe restrictions on the activities of any Christian group except for the Church of England. Baptists, among others, were unable to meet legally for worship. The Confession's title page says that it was 'put forth by the elders and brethren of many congregations of Christians (baptized upon profession of their faith) in London and the country', though they may not have actually met to approve the document.

It was not until September 1689, when the Toleration Act gave Dissenters (as they became known) some degree of religious freedom, that representatives of over a hundred Particular Baptist churches were able to meet freely in an assembly to recommend the Confession to their congregations. They thought it appropriate, they said:

> (for the satisfaction of all other Christians that differ from us in the point of Baptism) to recommend to their perusal the confession of our faith, which confession we own, as containing the doctrine of our faith and practice, and do

desire that the members of the churches respectively do furnish themselves therewith.

The assembly that met in 1689 did not itself publish the text of the Confession, possibly because an edition of the 1677 Confession had been published in the previous year. Hence there is no '1689' edition of the Second London Confession of Faith. Further editions were published in 1699, 1719 and 1720, after which interest in the Confession seems to have dipped.

The 1677/1689 Confession was not the first confession of faith of the Particular Baptists. In 1644, seven Particular Baptist churches in London issued a document setting out their core beliefs. They did this in response to attacks that were being made against the Baptist movement. They wanted to show to their opponents and to the world in general that their theology was biblically orthodox. They especially wanted to demonstrate that they were not Arminian, by distancing themselves from the General Baptists with whom they were often confused.

In response to further attacks, a second edition of the 1644 Confession was published in 1646. This edition strengthened the confession's calvinistic theology and clarified its statement on religious freedom. This first confession of faith having been produced in London, the 1677/89 Confession became known as the Second London Confession of Faith.

No historical document appears without a historical context and there is a very clear historical context for the 1689 Confession. In the 1640s, the Westminster Assembly had been called by Parliament to work on a statement of faith for the churches. The Assembly was dominated by Presbyterians and so the documents which it produced, including the Westminster Confession of Faith, became the confessional standards of Presbyterianism.

In 1658, representatives of Congregational churches in London and the surrounding region were invited to a conference at the Savoy Palace. The eventual result of this meeting was a congregationalist statement of faith known as the Savoy Declaration of Faith and Order. It is consciously modelled upon the Westminster Confession of Faith, often following precisely the wording of that earlier document, in order to demonstrate the unity of belief between Presbyterians and Congregationalists in many areas of doctrine.

A similar principle was followed by the Particular Baptists in the production of the 1677/89 Confession. While the 1689 Confession often mirrors the Westminster Confession, in several places the Baptists preferred to follow the text of the Savoy Confession where it differed from Westminster. And in the areas of baptism and church government, of course, the 1677/89 document goes its own way.

That this approach to the formulation of the document was deliberate can be seen from the preface to the 1677/89 Confession, entitled 'To the Judicious and Impartial Reader'. There the framers of the document explain their decision to 'retain the same *order*' as that of Westminster and Savoy and also, where the two earlier confessions agreed, 'to follow their example in making use of the very same words with them both' in those 'very many' articles with which they were also in agreement.

Their aim in so doing, they said, was to 'manifest our consent' with the Presbyterians and Congregationalists and with many other Protestant groups 'whose orthodox confessions have been published to the world'. They had no desire to invent new statements of faith where that was unnecessary in the light of work done by others: they had 'no itch to clog religion with new words', but much preferred to demonstrate their 'hearty agreement with them, in that wholesome Protestant doctrine, which with so clear evidence of Scriptures they have asserted'.

Their aim was to demonstrate unity with brethren from whom they differed on matters of church government and polity and, on those latter matters, to express their views clearly and unashamedly.

The 1689 Confession today

The popularity of the 1689 Confession has waxed and waned over the years. It seems to have fallen somewhat into disuse in the middle of the eighteenth century, before being reprinted in 1791. There followed a further period of neglect in the early nineteenth century, before Charles Spurgeon had the Confession reprinted in 1855, shortly after starting his ministry in London at New Park Street Chapel.

Less interest was shown in the Confession again over the first half of the twentieth century before renewed interest saw further reprints from 1958 onwards. Interest in recent years has been at a higher level again. It is noteworthy that the reprints have coincided with the revival of a love for the doctrines of grace: under Andrew Fuller and others in the late eighteenth century, under Spurgeon in the mid-nineteenth century and as a result of the ministry of Martyn Lloyd-Jones in the twentieth. The current enthusiasm for reformed doctrine has fuelled a revival of interest in the 1689 Confession in our own day.

Not everyone is persuaded, however, that a seventeenth-century statement of faith is a very useful document for the twenty-first century church. The objections most commonly heard are that the language is out-of-date, that the Confession addresses issues of 350 years ago and not the issues of today, that detailed confessions of faith divide Christians at a time when we need to be uniting and that we are better off learning directly from the divinely inspired Bible rather than through a man-made statement of faith.

In response, it may be said that the language, though sometimes difficult, can be understood with a little patient study (and modernised versions are available – see 'Further reading', below); that the Confession addresses, for the most part, timeless questions of biblical doctrine, not questions of only passing interest (though additional statements on current issues, for example in the areas of gender and sexuality, can also be helpful); that the aim of the Confession was to unite, not to divide, and so it deals with the core, foundational elements of Christian doctrine which simply reflect a Protestant reformed and baptistic understanding of biblical teaching; and that the Confession is intended to take a clearly subordinate place to Scripture, which is indeed our sole authority in questions of faith and life.

A detailed confession of faith, such as the 1689 Confession, is in fact an extremely helpful document in both church life and in the life of the individual believer today. For a church to have the 1689 Confession as its basis of faith indicates clearly where it stands on important questions of doctrine and church life: it explains what the church believes the Bible to teach on fundamental questions and provides a means of safeguarding the soundness of what is actually taught in the church.

To have a historic statement of faith such as the 1689 Confession is important also as indicating continuity with past generations of believers: the church today has not concocted a set of beliefs on its own without reference to others but is self-consciously and verifiably connecting itself with fellow-Christians of former ages. A detailed statement of faith is, finally, a useful teaching tool within the church, both for instructing believers in the central truths of the faith and for helping to identify and refute error, should it arise in the life of the church.

Structure of the Confession

The 1689 Confession is made up of thirty-two chapters. It is introduced by a preface, 'To the Judicious and Impartial Reader', and, in its original printing, has an Appendix explaining the churches' reasons for holding to a different position on baptism from that of their paedobaptist brethren. Scripture references are given throughout the Confession to demonstrate the biblical nature of the truths that it affirms.

The chapters of the Confession are not thrown together randomly, but are carefully ordered in accordance with a clear, logical structure. The Confession begins in its first five chapters with the foundations of the doctrines of Scripture and of God. Scripture is the divine revelation on which everything in the Confession is based and, of course, everything (sin only excepted) originates with God. Chapters 2 to 5 thus deal in turn with God and the Trinity, God's decree, creation and providence.

The creation of man is dealt with in chapter 4 and so, after laying these foundations, the Confession turns to the spiritual condition of humanity by addressing the fall of man in chapter 6 and then the work of redemption in chapters 7 to 20. God's work of saving his people thus forms a major portion of the Confession, as would be expected. This section begins with the covenant as the foundation of all God's saving dealings with the human race (chapter 7) and the person and work of Christ as the lynchpin and central focus of the entirety of the work of salvation (chapter 8).

The Confession then moves on to consider (in chapters 9 to 20) all the principal aspects of Christ's work of salvation. First, redemption is considered from the perspective of God's initiative and work (chapters 9 to 13): free will, effectual calling, justification, adoption, sanctification; then it examines (in chapters 14 to 20) the manner in which God's work of salvation is received: saving faith, repentance, good works, perseverance, assurance, the law and the gospel.

The next major section of the Confession addresses Christian living and the life of the church (chapters 21 to 30). This, again, is entirely logical: God's work of salvation is prior to the Christian life and the church. Without redemption in Christ, it would be impossible for us to live as Christians and the church would not exist. This section addresses in turn Christian liberty, worship, oaths and vows, civil government, marriage, the church, Christian fellowship, and, in chapters 28 to 30, the ordinances.

The emphasis upon the church is unmistakeable and demonstrates the importance rightly given to that body in the rather less individualistic times in which the Confession was composed. The final two chapters of the Confession address eschatological (end-of-the-age) issues: the post-mortem state and the resurrection (chapter 31) and the last judgement (chapter 32).

The Confession, in common with its sister confessions of the seventeenth-century Protestant reformation in England, encompasses the teaching of the Bible on Scripture itself and the doctrine of God, through his work of redemption and its outworking in human life to the last things. It is, as B. B. Warfield put it in his discussion of the Westminster Confession of Faith, 'architectonic' in its conception. It covers the grand sweep of biblical revelation.

The 1689 Confession provides a solid, scriptural foundation and framework for the understanding of Christian doctrine and for living the Christian life. It repays careful study; I hope that this book will provide a useful introduction and handbook for such study.

How to use this book

This book works its way through the Confession chapter by chapter consecutively. That is the best way to study the Confession. I have sought to group together chapters of the Confession that deal with closely related subjects, to aid comprehension. You will need a copy of the Confession to hand as you read this book and you will make the most of the book if you refer frequently to the text of the Confession under discussion. I have quoted from the original text of the Confession, lightly updated for punctuation, capitalisation and spelling, with an occasional explanation (in square brackets) of out-moded or unfamiliar expressions.

You should also look up the Bible verses that the Confession refers to – occasionally, it is not immediately clear why a particular verse is cited, in which case the more detailed studies of the Confession referred to here in the next section may be of help. I have also included Bible references in my exposition of the

Confession, to help highlight how the teaching of the Confession is firmly rooted in Scripture.

The study questions at the end of each chapter are designed to stimulate your thinking and can be used whether you are studying the Confession on your own or with others – they are particularly designed for the use of church groups.

If you want to take your study of the Confession further and deeper, as I hope you will, the 'Further reading' section at the end of this chapter lists books that examine the text of the 1689 in more detail than is possible in this shorter volume.

If you want to go further in your study of the individual doctrines covered by the Confession, I have supplied some suggestions for further reading at the end of each chapter. These are not necessarily easy reading, but will repay careful study by stretching, challenging and expanding your understanding of the doctrines that they address.

Study questions

1. Read the 1689 Confession through. What is your overall impression? Are there things in it that surprised you, puzzled you, challenged you?

2. How could the Confession be helpful to your church, or to you personally? What pitfalls might need to be avoided in using it? What would be a good way of making use of it in church life?

3. What are some of the advantages and disadvantages of a more detailed confession of faith, such as the 1689 Confession, compared with the shorter statements of faith which many churches today adopt?

Further reading

As well as the original text, there are also available:

A *Faith to Confess: The Baptist Confession of Faith of 1689 Rewritten in Modern English*, 3rd edn. (Haywards Heath: Carey Publications, 1979)

The Baptist Confession of Faith, 1689: Updated English with Notes, Peter Masters, ed. (London: Wakeman Trust, 1998), though note that this version, following Charles Spurgeon's 1855 edition, omits the word 'Elect' at the start of Chapter 10.3.

James M. Renihan has provided a very useful brief guide to the study of the historic Protestant reformed confessions, particularly the 1689 Confession, in his *A Toolkit for Confessions: Helps for the Study of English Puritan Confessions of Faith* (Palmdale, CA: Institute of Reformed Baptist Studies, 2017).

Three in-depth and detailed expositions of and commentaries on the 1689 Confession are available:

Samuel E. Waldron, *A Modern Exposition of the 1689 Baptist Confession of Faith*, 5th edn. (Leyland: Evangelical Press, 2016)

Rob Ventura, ed., *A New Exposition of The London Baptist Confession of Faith of 1689* (Fearn: Christian Focus, 2022)

James M. Renihan, *Confessing the Faith. Vol. 2, The Second London Baptist Confession of Faith* (Macclesfield: Broken Wharfe, 2022), published in the USA as *To the Judicious and Impartial Reader: Baptist Symbolics, Volume 2, An Exposition of the 1689 London Baptist Confession of Faith* (Cape Coral, FL: Founders Press, 2023).

On the broader question of the usefulness of detailed confessions of faith, see:

J. V. Fesko, *The Need for Creeds Today: Confessional Faith in a Faithless Age* (Grand Rapids, MI: Baker Academic, 2020)

Carl R. Trueman, *The Creedal Imperative* (Wheaton, IL: Crossway, 2012)

Chapter 1:
Holy Scripture

On 18th April, 1521, a large hall in the city of Worms was crowded with the cream of the German nobility. Senior scholars and churchmen were there and, most impressive of all, presiding over the assembly was the Emperor, Charles V. Late in the afternoon, following the conclusion of other business, a rough-looking man with a bad haircut was brought in. He wore the plain black cassock of the Augustinian order of friars. On a table in front of him was a pile of books, of which he was the author. He was asked if he stood by what he had written in the books. In response, Martin Luther gave one of the most stirring affirmations of Christian liberty in the history of the church: 'I am bound by the Scriptures I have quoted and my conscience is captive to the word of God. I cannot and will not retract anything, since it is neither safe nor right to go against conscience.'[1]

---

1   See Lindal Roper, *Martin Luther: Renegade and Prophet* (London: Vintage, 2016), pp. 180, 183.

The principle on which Luther took his stand was one of the foundational principles of the reformation: *sola Scriptura* – the Bible alone is the authority for all Christian teaching. The opening chapter of the 1689 Confession begins with a resounding affirmation of this principle: 'The Holy Scripture is the only sufficient, certain, and infallible rule of all saving knowledge, faith and obedience'. It summarises in one pithy statement much of what the remainder of the chapter expounds. We can best grasp its teaching by asking a series of questions which its various paragraphs answer in turn.

Why do we need the Bible? (paragraph 1)

We all need clear, authoritative teaching on spiritual questions. This is provided by the Bible. In words that are original to the 1689 Confession, its opening affirmation, quoted above, makes clear that no merely human document can be set alongside – let alone supersede or take the place of – the Bible as the authoritative document of the Christian faith. All that we need is there, to teach and guide us in the knowledge of God and of his ways. No new revelation may be expected, nor is it required.

Like the Apostle Paul in the first chapter of his letter to the Romans, the Confession asserts that humanity has some knowledge of spiritual matters by virtue of God's general revelation. This revelation comes in two forms: firstly, the 'light of nature', by which the Confession means the residual knowledge that we have about spiritual things, even as fallen creatures, because we are made in the image of God. This would include basic ideas about the existence and nature of God and moral right and wrong. Secondly, general revelation comes through 'the works of creation and providence'.

These works are visible to humanity and ought to lead us to know enough about God's 'goodness, wisdom and power' as to leave us without excuse before him (Rom. 1:19–20; 2:14–15).

Neither the light of nature nor general revelation, however, teaches us 'that knowledge of God and his will, which is necessary unto salvation'. That is why we need the Bible. Here, then, is the twofold knowledge of God, of which reformed writers so often spoke: general revelation teaches God as creator, but only special revelation – the Scriptures – teaches God as redeemer (2 Tim. 3:15).

The Confession makes clear how the Bible came into being. Initially, God gave revelation to his people by various means – we could think of visions and dreams, the tablets of stone given at Sinai or even Ezekiel's dramatic representations, as well as the oracles of the prophets. The Confession goes on, however, to tell us that, 'for the more sure establishment, and comfort of the Church', God caused the entirety of his special revelation to be committed to writing.

It is this special revelation committed to written form – the Holy Scriptures – which is 'the only sufficient, certain, and infallible rule of all saving knowledge, faith and obedience', as paragraph 1 states. And because we now have in the Bible the whole of God's special revelation, all other forms of such revelation have 'now ceased'.

What is the Bible? (paragraphs 2 & 3)

This leads logically to the question, of what do the Scriptures consist? If they are the only sure guide to matters of salvation, we need to be absolutely sure that we have the right content, for fear that we will otherwise be led astray.

This is an important question today, when sects and cults want to add their own 'scriptures' to the Bible as authoritative and inspired. It was a central issue in the reformation, too, as the Bible used by the Roman Catholic Church for many centuries included the Apocrypha. Thus the Confession itemises (paragraph 2) each of the sixty-six books which make up the Old and New Testaments, as Protestants recognise them today (see Lk. 24:44; Jn.10:35). The list ends with the brief but vital statement, 'all which are given by the inspiration of God, to be the rule of faith and life' (see 2 Tim. 3:16).

So as to be clear about the status of the Apocrypha, the Confession goes on to assert (paragraph 3) that the books of the Apocrypha lack divine inspiration and so do not form part of the canon of scripture: they 'are of no authority to the Church of God' and should be used only in the same way as other, merely human, writings.

Why should we believe the Bible? (paragraphs 4 & 5)

Can we trust the Bible? How can we be sure that it is God's word? This is one of the key questions in our time. For many unbelievers, the question is hardly worth asking, as they assume that the Bible has been proven false in many different ways. This adds pressure to the believer who may be questioned about their beliefs, or may be entertaining doubts about the reliability of the Scriptures.

In response, we often argue from the correspondence of the Bible's accounts with what is known from other sources; or from the elevated lifestyle that the Bible teaches; or from the high level of spirituality that it promotes; or from the testimony of the church; or from other aspects of the Bible's content, or even style, which may recommend it to us. These and other factors are mentioned in the Confession (paragraph 5) as good subsidiary arguments as to why we should believe the Bible to be God's word, but they are emphatically not the first reason given for that purpose. Rather, the Confession asserts that the Bible is to be believed and received as the word of God on the authority of God himself as its author (paragraph 4; see Jn. 16:13–14).

The question then arises as to how we know this to be true: if it is indeed the case that God is the author of Scripture, then clearly it ought to be believed and received as such, but how can we be sure of this? The answer that the Confession provides may initially prove unsettling: God himself testifies to his own authorship by the 'inward work of the Holy Spirit, bearing witness by and with the word in our hearts' (paragraph 5).

We may find this hard to accept at first, because we are used to testing truth claims by external evidence that we believe we can assess objectively for ourselves. We have been taught that 'man is the measure of all things' and so want to use science or our own experience or knowledge to test the accuracy or credibility of anything. But that cannot work when we are dealing with revelation from heaven: our knowledge and experience, by definition, cannot test this, because it is beyond our ability to attain it for ourselves – that is why it has to be given to us by God himself.

How then does the Holy Spirit bring us to assurance about the divine authorship and authority of Scripture? We need to be clear that the Confession does not lead us to expect some kind of internal whisper, as we contemplate the Scriptures, telling us, 'This is really God's word.' Nor is some extraordinary feeling or sensation intended.

What is meant is that, as we read and meditate upon God's word, we will have the fundamental conviction in our minds and hearts that this is indeed the word of God. We will have come to that conviction in a variety of different ways, but it is the sovereign work of the Spirit to bring us to that conviction (1 Jn. 2:20, 27). And as we go on in our Christian lives and grow in grace, we may expect that conviction also to grow and become more settled and sure.

How then do we persuade others, especially unbelievers, to trust the Bible as God's word? Simply to tell them that we are so persuaded is unlikely to help. We may well invoke some of the factors mentioned above for this purpose. But above all, we will seek to bring to bear upon them the actual teaching of Scripture and will pray that, as the truths of God's word are applied to their minds and hearts, the Spirit will also do his work in them to bring them to the same conviction that we have.

What does the Bible teach? (paragraph 6)

The Bible does not tell us everything about everything: it will not teach you how to design a house or build an engine or make a dress or write computer code or understand Sanskrit. We must not try to draw from it lessons in areas that it does not set out to address. So the Confession makes clear that the Bible contains 'the whole counsel of God' about 'all things necessary for his own glory, man's salvation, faith and life' (paragraph 6). This informs us, in a brief summary, what is the scope of the teaching of Scripture: it is concerned with questions about God and salvation (2 Tim. 3:15–17).

We must always keep this in mind when we study the Bible and not try to make it teach matters outside its stated scope. We must note too that Scripture's teaching is limited to what is 'necessary' for us to know about these matters. God does not satisfy mere curiosity and so does not tell us, for example, why evil was allowed into the world or precisely how to reconcile his absolute sovereignty with human free agency or, indeed, very much about the detail of what it will be like to live in the new heavens and the new earth. The Bible contains all the teaching that we need to know 'that the man of God may be complete, equipped for every good work' (2 Tim. 3:17). Commentaries, books of theology and other aids are useful to help us come to a true understanding of Scripture, but they elucidate its teaching and do not add to it.

The Confession also makes clear (paragraph 6) that we are not to look anywhere else for authoritative statements on these matters: Scripture, in matters relating to God and salvation, is sufficient. At the time of the formulation of the reformed confessions, those faithful to the Scriptures faced two challenges which are still with us today. On the one hand were those who claimed that they received further revelation by the Holy Spirit, direct from heaven. They were generally referred to as 'enthusiasts'. There are those today who hold to this view. On the other hand was the Roman Catholic Church, which claimed authoritative status for its own unwritten traditions, as it still does.

The Confession makes clear that neither of these is an authoritative source of revelation and that all God's special revelation is contained in the sixty-six books of the Old and New Testaments and nowhere else.

How are we to understand the Bible?
(paragraphs 6, 7 & 9)

If the Bible, and the Bible alone, is God's word, we need to know what it means. How do we safely arrive at the true meaning of Scripture? The question is particularly acute because different people seem to arrive at very different understandings of it: Protestants and Roman Catholics, liberals and evangelicals, charismatics and cessationists (who believe that some or all of the gifts of the Spirit referred to, for example, in 1 Cor. 12 – 14, have now ceased), to name just a few. The Confession makes clear that there is only one true meaning of Scripture, not several (as some earlier theologians had asserted). So it sets out a number of principles which are to guide us in reaching a proper understanding of the teaching of the Bible.

Firstly, it is asserted (paragraph 7) that Scripture is clear. Although some parts of the Bible are indeed difficult to understand (see 2 Pet. 3:16), Scripture is crystal clear on the essentials: 'those things which are necessary to be known, believed, and observed for salvation'. Everyone, if they use the available means, can understand the teaching of the Bible on these matters.

This is indeed what we find in practice: charismatic and cessationist evangelicals, for example, differ on important matters concerning the work of the Holy Spirit in the life of the believer, but, as evangelicals, generally find themselves to be united in their understanding of the essentials of the gospel message. That is because both groups, on the whole, look to Scripture alone for their understanding of the fundamentals of the faith and, studying God's word honestly and with the help of the Holy Spirit, they arrive at the same or very similar conclusions on these fundamentals.

This is not the case, in contrast, for evangelical Protestants and Roman Catholics, or indeed for evangelical as opposed to liberal Protestants. In these cases, the problem is not that the Bible is unclear; rather, it is that other sources of authority besides the Bible have come in – tradition and the papacy in the case of Roman Catholics and human reasoning in the case of liberal Protestants – leading to different conclusions, even on gospel essentials.

Secondly, no one will come to a true 'saving understanding' of the teaching of the Bible without the help of the Holy Spirit. We need his 'inward illumination' (paragraph 6) for this (1 Cor. 2:11–12). Our minds are darkened because we are fallen creatures; and so we do not grasp the true meaning and implications of God's word unless God by his Spirit renews our minds and grants us light to enable us to understand. We should pray for this light whenever we come to the Bible, whether to read it for ourselves or to hear it preached or taught. Without the illumination of the Holy Spirit, we will go astray.

Thirdly, we are to use what the chapter calls 'ordinary means' (paragraph 7) to help our understanding: we may not presume upon the help of the Spirit so that we become lazy and refuse to use our God-given mind, knowledge and understanding. We are to search Scripture for the truth, because what may be unclear in one part of the Bible may well be more clearly stated in another part. And we are to compare one passage of Scripture with others, to ensure that we are not misunderstanding or distorting its true meaning (paragraph 9).

Biblical teaching does not always lie on the surface of the text of Scripture and so we need to think about the clear implications of what the Bible says on a particular matter – what the Confession says is 'necessarily contained' in Scripture (paragraph 6) – not only its express teaching. We are well advised to make use of other resources, in particular the preaching of our own pastor, to help us reach a proper understanding of the Bible, but we must always operate on the principle, as the Confession puts it, that 'the infallible rule of interpretation of Scripture is the Scripture itself' (paragraph 9). No human authority exists that can give an infallible ruling on what the Bible means or teaches on a particular subject. The Bible itself is that authority.

Fourthly, the Confession makes clear that there are some matters, like the time at which the church meets for worship on the Lord's Day or the precise number of elders or deacons that a church appoints, where decisions have to be taken on the basis of 'the light of nature and Christian prudence' based on general biblical principles (paragraph 6). In other words, enlightened common sense and wisdom, rooted in the general teaching of Scripture, need to guide us in reaching decisions in those areas.

Which versions of the Bible are authentic? (paragraph 8)

At the time of the reformation, the Roman Catholic Church held that its Latin translation of the Bible (the 'Vulgate') was the only authorised version of Scripture. In some countries, the translation of the Bible into the language of the people was forbidden on pain of death – a penalty which the great and godly scholar and Bible translator William Tyndale paid in 1536, in exile, when he was strangled at the stake and his body burned.

In stark contrast, the Confession affirms, firstly, that the authentic text of Scripture is the Hebrew of the Old Testament (to which we might add by way of clarification the Aramaic in which a few small portions of it were originally written) and the Greek of the New Testament. It was in these languages, asserts the Confession, that the text of Scripture was divinely inspired and which God has, in his providence, preserved. It is to those original language texts, therefore, that we must ultimately appeal.

Nevertheless, the Confession makes clear that Scripture is to be translated into the ordinary language of all nations of the world, so that all may benefit from them and may worship the true God of the Bible in an acceptable manner. The work of Bible translation is thus both necessary and highly commendable.

Conclusion (paragraph 10)

This first chapter of the Confession ends with a resounding statement of the final authority of Scripture to settle all controversies and disputes. Whatever questions may arise about the matters that the Bible addresses in its teaching, it is the Bible itself that is to be the 'supreme judge' of them. All councils, decrees and opinions of men, however learned, ancient or revered, must be examined in the light of the teaching of Scripture and must bow to its final authority.

And so the believer may 'rest', as this final paragraph puts it, in what God's word says, 'the Holy Scripture delivered by the Spirit'. The Bible provides us with the final, authoritative and unchallengeable judgement on all matters to do with the Christian's faith and in that we may be completely confident.

How precious is the book divine,
by inspiration given!

Bright as a lamp its doctrines shine,

to guide our souls to heaven.

John Fawcett

Study questions

1. What authority should a confession of faith, such as the 1689 Confession, have in church life, in the light of paragraph 1 of this Chapter?

2. In the light of paragraph 5, what arguments might we use to try to persuade someone that the Bible is the word of God?

3. How useful or necessary is it to study the original languages of the Bible in order to understand it (paragraph 8)? Is the answer different for those called to preach and teach the Scriptures?

Further reading

Mark D. Thompson, *The Doctrine of Scripture: An Introduction* (Wheaton, IL: Crossway, 2022)

John Calvin, *Institutes of the Christian Religion* (1559), Book 1, chapters 1–8

Chapter 2:
God and the Holy Trinity

As we approach the subject of the nature of God himself, let us pause and remember who it is that we are considering. It is possible to consider the doctrine of God at a merely intellectual level. 'God' then becomes no more than an object of academic curiosity, to be dissected, analysed and debated. We may become absorbed in such an exercise, but if we are not also inspired with awe and reverence before the thrice-holy God, we will suffer harm and enjoy no real benefit.

John Calvin insisted that God cannot be truly known without piety: the knowledge of God 'should serve first to teach us fear and reverence'. As we study who God is and what he is like, we are to 'learn to seek every good from him and, having received it, to credit it to his account'.[1] As we approach this topic, therefore, may we be filled with a spirit of devotion to God and with true faith in him.

---

1   John Calvin, *Institutes of the Christian Religion* I.ii.2.

The teaching of chapter 2 of the 1689 Confession will sound very strange in the ears of many believers today. Much of it addresses aspects of the doctrine of God which have been largely forgotten, or even rejected. Whereas most evangelical churches would affirm chapter 1 of the Confession on the Scriptures, many may have considerable doubts about important aspects of chapter 2, or may simply never have heard them taught. This makes it all the more vital to study it and recover its biblical truths.

The attributes of God (paragraph 1)

We have a sinful tendency to think of God as just a larger, better version of ourselves. In contrast, chapter 2 of the Confession asserts that God is unique: he is the 'one only living and true God'; God is completely independent of anything and anyone else: 'whose subsistence is in and of himself'; he is infinite 'in being and perfection'; and he transcends all creation: 'whose essence cannot be comprehended by any but himself'. As Isaiah asks, 'With whom will you compare God?' (Is. 40:18).

We need urgently to recover a high view of God's majesty, glory and holiness. God is not our best mate; he is not an indulgent grandfather figure; he is not there simply to solve our problems and fulfil our sense of self. He is almighty God, who has no need of us, who is in no way limited by us in anything that he is or wishes to do and who is infinitely far beyond our ability to understand or grasp. 'For our God is a consuming fire' (Heb. 12:29). We need to learn again the biblical 'fear of the Lord'.

This sense of awe should be deepened by the brief phrases and single adjectives ascribed to God in this opening paragraph of chapter 2, which underline the scale of the difference between God and us. Where we are constantly changing, God is unchanging ('immutable'). We have a beginning and an end, but God is 'eternal'. We have bodies which limit us in time and space; God is 'a most pure spirit', not confined by space ('immense') or time ('every way infinite'). We are often foolish; God is 'most wise'. We are sinful creatures; God is 'most holy'. We are constrained in what we will and do; God is 'most free'. We cannot achieve half the things we would like to do; God works 'all things according to the counsel of his own immutable and most righteous will, for his own glory'. Look up the Bible verses supplied in paragraph 1 of chapter 2 and meditate on the divine attributes that it records. Such an exercise will bring us to our knees in worship.

Controversies

Judgement

Two aspects of the teaching of this paragraph are controversial today, even among evangelicals. Firstly, it states, in language that draws upon God's revelation of himself to Moses (Ex. 34:6–7), that God is 'most loving, gracious, merciful, long suffering, abundant in goodness and truth, forgiving iniquity, transgression and sin, the rewarder of them that diligently seek him'. Our God is a pre-eminently gracious God, as evidenced supremely in the giving of himself in the person of the Son to die on the cross for sinners.

That is not controversial, of course. It goes on, however, to assert that God is also 'terrible in his judgements, hating all sin, and who will by no means clear the guilty'. Although these words also reflect God's self-revelation to Moses (Ex. 34:7), they nevertheless represent themes that are less often heard in our churches today.

Why are we so reluctant to address this aspect of God, so clearly taught in Scripture? Partly, it is our sinful and darkened hearts and minds, which still recoil from the idea of divine judgement. A further factor is the mindset of our secular society. The contemporary emphasis upon the need to affirm each individual means that any suggestion of guilt or punishment is unacceptable.

Many believe that no one has the right to tell them what they should be or how they should behave. Even God is not permitted to infringe the individual's absolute right of self-determination. God then becomes no more than a facilitator of our enjoyments, to be blamed when life takes a bad turn. But if he is no more than that, what need is there of a Saviour crucified for sinners? The church needs urgently to recover the biblical teaching of God's holy hatred of sin.

'Without body, parts or passions'

The second aspect of the paragraph which is widely questioned by evangelicals today is the statement that God is 'without body, parts, or passions'. Few want to say that God has a body, but other aspects of this statement are questioned today. Firstly, God is 'without parts'. This means that he is entirely one and unified in his being. He cannot be divided up into different parts. Although we may speak of his various attributes, as Scripture does, he is not made up of his attributes nor can he be broken down into them. He is one, a unity. He is not a complex being made of various factors and characteristics, but entirely and simply one.

God is also 'without passions' (impassible). At the time of the Confession, this statement was entirely uncontroversial. In recent years, some effort has been made, firstly, to understand what is meant when we affirm God's impassibility and, secondly, to persuade believers that such an affirmation is biblical and true. Let us address the issue with some brief comments that may help to dispel some of the myths which surround this question.

Defenders of divine impassibility do not believe that God is cold, like a stone, and lacking in love. Rather, the doctrine of impassibility counters the idea that God's love is simply a bigger and better version of human love. As we have seen, this is in accord with one of the principal objectives of this chapter of the Confession.

The doctrine teaches that God is not like us, constantly changing in our loves, joys, dislikes and hates. He is always fully and entirely who he is in all eternity and is not subject to change as a result of external events or of anything in himself. He is consistently full of love and joy, for example, in a way that is entirely perfect and good, free from the sin, weakness and change which mar human feelings. And he is consistently and fully opposed in his whole being to sin, which the Bible often describes in terms of his wrath.

The doctrine of divine impassibility is thus, in one sense, simply an aspect of God's immutability (that is, he does not change). What then of language in the Bible that seems to teach that God does change, for example that he repents (1 Sam. 15:11, 35) or experiences inner emotional turmoil (Hos. 11:8–9)? The short response is that the Bible is here speaking to us in language that we can understand, but does not ascribe to God literal changes of attitude or feeling – just as the Bible speaks of God's arm, hand and eye, but does not expect us to believe that he literally has any actual body parts.

Why do believers today find this doctrine so difficult? Part of the answer lies in the response of some theologians, notably Jürgen Moltmann, to the terrible suffering of the Second World War and, in particular, the Holocaust. To the question, where is God in such terrible experiences, many have felt that the only honest reply was that God suffered alongside the sufferers.

This response may be reinforced when we consider how to comfort those who have, for example, lost a beloved daughter to a ravaging cancer. We may want to tell them God is moved by their suffering and shares in it. A further factor is the enormous importance that our society places on feelings. Our attitudes to ourselves and to others are strongly influenced by how we feel. This leads to an assumption that something similar must also be true of God.

Comfort for the suffering is of course vital to the Christian faith. Our feelings are not ignored in Scripture. True comfort, however, and a true understanding of the nature of God flow only from biblical teaching, however strange or unpalatable that teaching might at first seem. We must therefore take seriously those verses which proclaim that God does not change (Mal. 3:6; Jas. 1:17), including in his love (1 Jn. 4:8), in his blessedness (1 Tim. 6:15) and in his hatred of sin (Ps. 7:11; Rom. 1:18).

Those who formulated the confessions of faith of the seventeenth century were persuaded that the Bible thus reveals to us a God who is impassible and that it is, in fact, only such a God who provides true comfort to those who mourn. He is always all-wise and all-powerful, full of mercy and grace. It is, moreover, this God who took human flesh and suffered and died for sinners.

Those who teach that God is without passions also strongly affirm that the Lord Jesus Christ experienced all kinds of human feelings and sufferings, without sin, and is therefore able to sympathise with us in our suffering (Heb. 2:18; 4:15). It is here that any reservations that we might harbour on this subject are fully and finally resolved. No one, on the last day, will be able justly to accuse God of not knowing how it feels to suffer as a human.

God's self-existence (paragraph 2)

The main thrust of the second paragraph of chapter 2 is, like the subjects just discussed, unpalatable to modern ears. It teaches that God does not depend upon humanity for his existence or actions, that he is utterly sovereign in all that he does and that he regards his own glory as the highest good.

In contrast, we like to imagine that we are inherently rather important to God, that we have some ability to act entirely independently of his will and that our good is at least as important as God's glory, if not more so. On all these points, our thinking may well need serious adjustment in the light of the teaching of this paragraph.

Firstly, then, God is independent of us and of all his creation: he is 'alone in and unto himself all-sufficient, not standing in need of any creature', for he has 'all life, glory, goodness, blessedness, in and of himself'. The Confession here cites Job 22:2–3, where Eliphaz asks Job, 'Can a man be of any use to God? Can even a wise man be of use to him? Does it delight the Almighty if you are righteous? Does he profit if you perfect your behaviour?'

The book of Job is an object lesson in the Lord's utter independence of man, as God's speeches to Job from chapter 38 onwards demonstrate. When Paul describes God as 'the blessed and only Sovereign' (1 Tim. 6:15), marvels at 'the depth of the riches and the wisdom and the knowledge of God', or cries out, 'How unsearchable his judgements and untraceable his ways' (Rom. 11:33), he is awe-struck at God's all-sufficiency in himself and in the Lord's utter freedom from dependence upon anyone else at all.

The paragraph, secondly, goes on to affirm that God has 'most sovereign dominion over all creatures, to do by them, for them, or upon them, whatsoever himself pleaseth'. We are all his and so he has every right to rule us. He consults no one; he relies on none other for advice; he needs information or wisdom from no other source. God does precisely as he sees fit.

Again, this is not a popular idea. We like to feel that we have some real say in what occurs. And of course we do, but only in a secondary sense. Our decisions, though the decisions of free agents, are subject to the sovereign will of God, who is the first cause of all things. This offends our pride and sense of significance, but it is the clear teaching of the Bible (Prov. 19:21; Is 46:10; Eph. 1:11). We must bow before our sovereign God.

Thirdly, God gains no glory from his creation, 'only manifesting his own glory in, by, unto, and upon them'. God's glory, not ours, is the highest good, as Paul affirms: 'For from him and through him and to him are all things. To him be the glory for ever. Amen.' (Rom. 11:36). The Bible everywhere ascribes all glory to God and repudiates all human claims to it.

Once more, we do not like this, as fallen humanity wants to claim glory for itself. Yet it is only right that God should act for his own glory, because he is truly glorious. For this reason, the paragraph ends with a call to all angels and all humanity to give God 'whatsoever worship, service or obedience as creatures they owe unto the Creator, and whatever he is further pleased to require of them'.

Our triune God (paragraph 3)

The final paragraph of chapter 2 addresses the doctrine of the Trinity. There is controversy here as well, for some evangelicals. We all need to ask how deeply ingrained in our thought, life and worship is the triune nature of God. How often do we hear, or maybe voice, expressions which confuse the three persons of the Godhead (addressing the Father as the one who died on the cross, for example), treat one person as if he were simply an alternative form of another (as if the Son or the Spirit were simply the Father performing different roles in his creative or redemptive work), or only ever address the deity with the word 'God'? We all express ourselves badly from time to time, perhaps particularly in this area, but a greater understanding of the trinitarian truths that the church has confessed for centuries would help us speak more biblically both to and about our glorious God.

The paragraph affirms, in line with historic Christian orthodox teaching as encapsulated in the early Christian creeds, that there are in the Godhead three 'subsistences': the framers of the Confession avoided the more usual term 'person', perhaps for fear of confusion with the everyday meaning of that word. The three are identified as the Father, the Word (or Son) and the Holy Spirit.

The paragraph then makes the vital claim that each of these three has 'the whole divine essence, yet the essence undivided'. In other words, each of the three persons is fully God. The Father is not more 'God' than the Son or the Spirit. We are not to think that there is some kind of 'real God' behind Christ the Son, for the Son is fully God. Neither the Son nor the Spirit is some kind of subordinate deity. At the same time, God is not made up of three parts. He is indivisible and one. We cannot fully grasp these truths with our finite minds, yet from Scripture we can see that they are true.

The paragraph goes on to tell us how each of the three persons is distinguished from, yet related to, the others. The Father 'is of none, neither begotten nor proceeding', whereas the Son 'is eternally begotten of the Father', the Spirit 'proceeding from the Father and the Son'. This is standard trinitarian teaching, but has, again, proved controversial in more recent times. Some have questioned whether we can be so precise about the distinctions and relations between the three persons of the Godhead.

In our day, the idea that the Son is eternally begotten has come under attack by some prominent evangelical theologians. Partly this is due to a right sense of our utter inability to comprehend God, but partly also from a neglect of the historic teaching of the church and from (I believe) some misunderstanding of what precisely is taught and how it is derived from Scripture. In brief, we say that the Son is eternally begotten of the Father to express the truth that the Father is always the Father and the Son is always the Son: the Father-Son relationship in the Godhead is real and eternal.

The chapter ends with a wonderful expression of the experiential value of the doctrine of the Trinity: it is 'the foundation of all our communion with God and comfortable dependence on him'. This expression derives from the Savoy Declaration of Faith and Order, in the drafting of which John Owen was deeply involved. It was Owen who wrote a substantial treatise on communion with God, expounding at length the unusual topic of the various ways in which the believer enjoys communion with each of the three persons of the Trinity (*Of Communion with God the Father, Son, and Holy Ghost,* to be found in volume 2 of Owen's works reprinted by Banner of Truth). It reminds us that our fellowship is not with some monadic, impersonal, far away god, but with the God and Father of our Lord Jesus Christ, by the Holy Spirit.

> Holy, holy, holy, Lord God almighty!
> early in the morning our song shall rise to Thee;
> holy, holy, holy! merciful and mighty,
> God in three Persons, blessèd Trinity.
>
> Reginald Heber

Study questions

1. Select in turn one or more of the attributes of God listed in paragraph 1 of chapter 2, look up the Scripture references and meditate reverently on them, reflecting on how these attributes are manifested perfectly, infinitely and originally in God.

2. How do the truths of paragraph 2 lead us to (a) worship God, (b) trust in him and (c) receive comfort from him?

3. Consider how essential the doctrine of the Trinity is (a) to our evangelism and (b) to our lives as Christian believers.

Further reading

Robert Letham, *The Holy Trinity: In Scripture, History, Theology, and Worship* (Phillipsburg, NJ: P&R, 2019)

Herman Bavinck, *The Doctrine of God*, trans. W. Hendriksen (Edinburgh: Banner of Truth, 1977)

John Owen, *Of Communion with God the Father, Son, and Holy Ghost* in Owen, *Works*, vol. 2 (repr., Edinburgh: Banner of Truth, 1965)

Samuel D. Renihan, *God Without Passions: The Majesty of God's Unshakeable Perfection* (Broken Wharfe, 2024)

Chapters 3 – 5:
God's Decree & Works

The biblical doctrine of the sovereignty of God gives great comfort and strength to God's people. Paradoxically, it has also given rise to confusion and dismay for some. The section of the 1689 Confession considered here – chapters 3, 4 and 5 – teaches that God both created and controls all things.

Many Christians have struggled to understand how this works out in life. If God controls everything, what do we say when a friend's daughter is tragically killed in a road accident or a work colleague contracts a terminal illness? More broadly, if God controls everything, where does that leave human free will? Why did God permit sin to enter the world in the first place? And if God is at the root of everything, how do we avoid the conclusion that sin, too, is his responsibility?

Some worry about the doctrine of election: if we teach that certain individuals were chosen by God before creation to be saved and others are predestined to be lost in hell for ever, what motivation is there for evangelism? And on what basis do we urge people to repent and trust in Christ? After all, if they are elect, they will be saved and, if not, there is nothing that anyone can do about it.

These are important questions and raise legitimate concerns. Christians are not helped, however, when churches' teaching in these areas is deficient. A failure to communicate clearly what Scripture teaches on this topic will harm the faith of God's people. Such an approach weakens evangelism, muffles the call to repentance and faith in Christ and robs believers of the ability to provide real comfort to those who suffer terrible tragedy in their lives.

For these reasons, the retrieval and reappropriation of the doctrines taught in chapters 3, 4 and 5 of the 1689 Confession is urgently needed. Our seventeenth-century forefathers understood these issues very clearly. We would do well to give time and thought to study the doctrine as they formulated it in these chapters.

The decree of God (chapter 3, paragraphs 1 & 2)

The fundamental principles that underlie all three chapters under consideration are set out in the first paragraph of chapter 3, 'Of God's Decree'. The following essential points are established:

- God's decree is 'from all eternity'. That is to say, it was not made in time, either at or after creation. Like God himself, the divine decree lies outside time (Eph. 1:4, 11).
- God consulted no one about his decree, but simply decreed 'in himself'. This phrase emphasises that the decree is the decree of God, according to 'his own will' and not that of any other, a will that is characterised by his 'most wise and

holy counsel'. We can be sure, then, that everything in God's decree is entirely in line with the character of God: so it is good, true, righteous, holy and wise and manifests his mercy, love and grace, as well as his wrath against sin (Is. 46:9–13; Eph. 1:5).

- God's decree is all-embracing: it covers 'whatsoever comes to pass'. Nothing is left out. Even things that we may regard as bad are covered by God's decree. Because such a statement is open to misunderstanding, four points of clarification are immediately made in the opening paragraph:
  - ♦ God is not the author of sin
  - ♦ God has no fellowship with anyone in sin
  - ♦ human will is not violated
  - ♦ 'second causes' are real causes, albeit subsidiary to the first cause which is the decree of God.

One further clarification is supplied in paragraph 2: God's decree is not based on his foresight of the future. Although he knows everything that will happen, as well as everything that would have happened under different conditions, his foresight did not determine his decree. Rather, it is the decree that has determined what will happen. God's decree is primary, not his foresight (Rom. 9:11–13).

Predestination, eternal life and damnation (chapter 3, paragraphs 3 to 7)

The remainder of chapter 3 explains how the decree works out in the predestination of some to eternal life and in the condemnation of others. The focus of these paragraphs is very firmly on election to life, without neglecting the question of judgement.

Angels as well as humans are predestined (1 Tim. 5:21): 'some men and angels are predestinated or fore-ordained to eternal life' (paragraph 3). This happens 'through Jesus Christ to the praise of his glorious grace'. Election cannot be considered without reference to Christ (Eph. 1:3-14). The angels and humans who are predestined are definitively identified by the decree in advance. Their number is certain. The passing of time and the occurrence of events cannot affect this. God's decision to choose them rather than others was his alone and took no account of anything in the individuals so chosen. God's reasons for his choice are 'the secret counsel and good pleasure of his will' (paragraph 5).

This clear, unqualified teaching on the absolute nature of election to eternal life raises some questions. Firstly, where does this leave all the biblical commands to repent and believe on Christ for salvation? Why is there so much emphasis in Scripture on the need for sinners to turn from their sin and trust in Christ – something that clearly they are expected to do, in the exercise of their own wills – if it is all settled in advance by God's eternal decree?

The chapter deals with this: God has appointed the means by which the elect will be saved, as well as the end result (paragraph 6). So the redemption, effectual calling, justification, adoption, sanctification and perseverance of the elect for their salvation also form part of God's eternal decree (Rom. 8:29-30). This covers both the work of Christ in saving his people and the work of the Holy Spirit in bringing the elect to faith in Christ and empowering them to persevere to the end.

What is emphasised here, then, is that salvation is all of God. With the exception of elect infants dying in infancy and those other 'elect persons, who are incapable of being outwardly called by the ministry of the word' (chapter 10, paragraph 3), the elect must come to saving faith in Christ and persevere in that faith until they die if they are to be saved. God's decree ensures that this will certainly be the case for every one of the elect (and for no one else). God's decree cannot fail.

It is the absolute nature of the decree that underpins and motivates our evangelism. A fully biblical understanding of the plight of the sinner sees the hopelessness of the case without God. We come into this world as sinners; our thoughts and desires, words and actions are entirely under the power of sin; we are blind to the truth and we are dead in sin. There is no way that we can help ourselves or one another out of this desperate condition. The most powerful evangelism in the world will do nothing to move us to saving faith in Christ, if it is not made effective by the power of God exercised through the Holy Spirit (Jn. 6:44).

Once we realise this, we see what a tremendous incentive it is to evangelism that God has decreed to save some, predestinating them to eternal life without regard to anything in them (Rom. 9:11). The result is that, as the gospel is preached, the elect will infallibly respond, at some point, with true repentance and faith and become followers of Christ (Jn. 10:27; 17:20, 24). This is tremendously good news. Without it, all our evangelistic efforts would be doomed.

A second question concerns the application of God's decree to those who are lost. Are we really to believe that, just as God has elected some to eternal life, so he has predestined others to eternity in hell? That sounds unbelievably cruel and unjust, so much so that many who teach a fixed decree of election to life refuse to hold anything similar in regard to those who are lost.

How does the Confession handle this? It says very little on the subject, confining itself to the simple statement that those who are not elected to life have been 'left to act in their sin to their condemnation, to the praise of his glorious justice' (paragraph 3). While the cause of election to life is in God alone and not in any way in the sinner, the opposite is the case for those who are lost. In the words of the Westminster Confession of Faith, they are condemned 'for their sin' and are 'left to act in their sin'.

The idea here is that of passing by – God does not confer upon them the benefits of the grace and mercy which is given to the elect. Because it is grace, no one has any right to it and so no one may justly complain if they do not benefit from it. Ultimately, the lost will be in hell because of their sin.

Finally, the question arises as to how this teaching should be handled. The chapter is clear that it is a 'high mystery' and so needs to be 'handled with special prudence' (paragraph 7). This warning is necessary, for many of the difficulties that Christians (and others) have experienced with the doctrine of election stem from its being badly taught.

The chapter makes clear that the teaching of election should never lead to pride and complacency, but rather to 'humility, diligence and abundant consolation, to all that sincerely obey the gospel'. It should lead us to 'praise, reverence and admiration of God', as well as to an assurance of salvation as we give attention to 'the will of God revealed in his word' and yield obedience to it.

In other words, this doctrine must not lead us to try to peer into God's decree of election, which is secret. The identity of the elect is not revealed to us. We are not to expect a direct answer to the question, 'Am I (or is someone else) elect?' Rather, we are to give our attention to God's revealed will – the Scriptures – believing its promises, heeding its warnings and obeying its instructions. As we do so, believers find themselves increasingly 'assured of their eternal election' and the recipients of 'abundant consolation'.

The works of God (chapters 4 & 5)

The works of God are divided by the Confession into two categories – God's initial work of creation which was complete after the six days described in the first chapter of the book of Genesis and the work of providence which continues from the act of creation until the end of the world. The Confession addresses each in turn.

Creation

In a brief chapter of three paragraphs (chapter 4), the Confession sets out the essential teaching of the Bible on God's work of creation, especially as presented in the opening chapters of the book of Genesis. It presents the work as trinitarian, God-glorifying, universal, time-limited and very good (paragraph 1). The penultimate point is important: God's work of creation is finished – and it took six days.

It is also important to note that the work of creation covered 'all things, whether visible or invisible'. God's purpose in creating the world was his own glory, so that his power, wisdom and goodness might thereby shine forth. And all was made 'very good'. There was no fault or defect in it all, as created.

The rest of chapter 4 is given over to the creation of humanity. In our day of gender fluidity, it is vital to note that, as Scripture affirms, humanity was made in two genders only, male and female. No distinction is made between the concepts of gender and of sex. Humans were made with 'reasonable and immortal souls ... after the image of God, in knowledge, righteousness, and true holiness'. God's law was written in their hearts. Moreover, they were specially instructed not to eat of the tree of knowledge of good and evil.

They had the power to keep these laws and while they did so, 'they were happy in their communion with God'. They ruled over the rest of creation. Yet, as a hint of what was to come, the Confession (paragraph 2) affirms that they were 'yet under a possibility of transgressing': sin was an option for them, as God had left them 'to the liberty of their own will', which was changeable.

Providence

God's work of creation completed, his work of providence continues. Chapter 5 makes clear that this work covers everything that happens. By it, God 'doth uphold, direct, dispose and govern all creatures and things, from the greatest even to the least'. He does this as he sees fit, for his own glory and in accordance with 'his wisdom, power, justice, infinite goodness and mercy' (paragraph 1). Nothing happens by chance, for nothing happens apart from God's providence (paragraph 2).

This, like the decree itself, raises a number of questions, which the remainder of chapter 5 addresses. Firstly, there is the issue of 'second causes'. God's decree and his providence are the first cause of everything. Just as in his decree God ordained the means by which the elect will be saved as well as the end result, so with his providence he orders all things 'to fall out according to the nature of second causes'.

It is vital to grasp the place of second causes in the teaching of the chapter, for otherwise we become fatalists. The fatalist believes simply that 'what will be will be'. There is no point in looking left and right when you cross the road, because if you are going to be run over by a bus, that is what will happen and nothing you do (or do not do) will make any difference. This is not biblical teaching.

The Bible makes very clear that humans have responsibility and that they make decisions and choices which have real effects in the world. More broadly, it is clear from Scripture that (as we all know), one event really does cause another. If I swing a bat to bring it into contact with a ball, the ball will move. That is not coincidence. The two events are not unconnected. One causes the other. The causation is real: without my swinging the bat, there would have been no movement in the ball.

The Confession calls these causes 'second causes', to make clear that they are genuine causes, but that they are secondary to the first cause, which is the providence of God, without which no bat would swing and no ball move. First and second causes do not operate at the same level, as second causes are themselves completely dependent upon the first cause, God's providence. They are nevertheless true causes. Human decisions and actions are thus significant and have real effects. We are responsible creatures.

This raises the question of miracles and other supernatural events, where ordinary cause and effect appear not to apply. When Jesus cleansed a leper or raised Lazarus from the dead, it is clear that something beyond the ordinary was occurring and that the usual rules that apply in our normal experience were not the cause.

Similarly, when the shadow went back by a certain number of hours for Hezekiah (2 Kgs. 20:11), or stood still for Joshua to win the battle (Jos. 10:13), usual modes of operation were suspended. The Confession allows for this, as it must in order to be true to Scripture, by making clear that God is 'free to work without, above and against' means 'at his pleasure' (paragraph 3).

Finally there is the question of sin. We know that God is not and cannot be the author of sin. How does this fit with the universal nature of his work of providence? The chapter is very careful in its answer to this, so as to hold these things together in a biblical manner. It does this in three ways.

- It makes clear that even sinful actions fall within the 'determinate counsel' of God. God did not merely give permission or allow the sinful action (paragraph 4). The acts which are sinful, considered purely as actions, are within the range of God's providence. Their sinful quality, however, belongs to the creature alone; God is not tainted with their sin in any way. This can be seen more starkly in Scripture when Peter describes the crucifixion of Christ. It was, he said, by 'God's determined plan and foreknowledge' that Christ was delivered to 'lawless people' who put him to death on the cross (Acts 2:23). The actions of the soldiers nailing Christ to the cross fell within the providence of God and were thus ordained by him. God sustained their physical strength and skill in wielding the hammer and the nails as they drove in Christ's flesh. But the hatred, injustice and cruelty of those who put him there and their desire to see him dead was not from God: it was the responsibility of Christ's enemies alone.

- The chapter also teaches that God sometimes leaves believers to the 'temptations and the corruptions of their own hearts' (paragraph 5). He does this to chastise and discipline them for their sins and to teach them something of the true nature of their hearts, so that they may be humbled, more watchful against sin in the future and more dependent upon the Lord for help and deliverance in temptation.

- The wicked and ungodly whom God would condemn for their sin are hardened by the Lord in their sin and find themselves given over in their lusts more and more to evil. Again, however, it is they alone who are responsible for their sin.

Chapter 5 ends by reminding us of the very comforting truth that God's providence is especially directed to the care of the church (paragraph 7). All that occurs in this world, ultimately, is for God's glory – and also for the good of his people. That is why believers may trust the Lord in all things, however bad or hard they may seem, knowing that their heavenly Father by his most wise providence controls and directs all things for their good.

A sovereign Protector I have,
    unseen, yet for ever at hand,
unchangeably faithful to save,
    almighty to rule and command.
He smiles, and my comforts abound;
    His grace as the dew shall descend;
and walls of salvation surround

the soul He delights to defend.

Augustus Montague Toplady

Study questions

1. What comfort does the teaching of these chapters bring to believers who suffer great tragedy in their lives?

2. How does the doctrine of creation affect your attitude to (a) the world around you, (b) your possessions and daily needs?

3. In what ways does the doctrine of election encourage you as a Christian and strengthen you in living for Christ?

4. Consider the value of noting how God by his providence works in the small as well as in the big things in your life.

Further reading

Samuel D. Renihan, *Deity and Decree* (Macclesfield: Broken Wharfe, 2021)

D. M. Lloyd-Jones, *God's Ultimate Purpose: An Exposition of Ephesians One* (Edinburgh: Banner of Truth, 1978)

John Flavel, *The Mystery of Providence* (repr., Edinburgh: Banner of Truth, 2021)

J. I. Packer, *Evangelism and the Sovereignty of God* (revd. edn., Leicester: IVP, 2010)

Chapters 6 & 7:
Human Sin and God's Covenant

Terrible wildfires burned in California in 2020. The Creek Fire near Shaver Lake, 200 miles east of San Francisco, is said to have been the largest single fire in the modern history of the state. Hundreds who were camping there for the Labor Day holiday that year woke in the middle of the night to find themselves trapped by blazing fires, unable to escape. Emergency services had to airlift them to safety. They had had no inkling of the danger they would be facing, as they drove to their holiday destination that weekend.

In the same way, but far more seriously, many have not the faintest realisation of the fearful condition into which humanity was plunged, when Adam and Eve ate from the tree of the knowledge of good and evil, forbidden to them by God on pain of death. Chapters 6 and 7 of the 1689 Confession show the depth and extent of the damage done to our condition by that first act of human disobedience; and then unfold the even greater grace of God in providing a remedy through the new covenant in Christ.

The Fall, Sin and Punishment (chapter 6)

Chapter 6 begins with a brief description of the fall of our 'first parents'. Paragraph 1 affirms the initial state of man, created 'upright and perfect'; God 'gave him a righteous law' which would have meant 'life had he kept it', yet 'threatened death' for breaking it. Sadly, it was not kept and was indeed broken. The Confession states, though without express biblical warrant, that it was 'not long' after their creation that Adam and Eve fell into sin. This appears to reflect earlier confessions on which the framers of the 1689 drew – the True Confession of 1596 states that the Fall occurred 'straight ways after' the creation of man (Article 4); and the First London Baptist Confession of 1644 states, 'long he [man] abode not in this honour' (Article IV).

Paragraph 1 goes on to state that Satan used the serpent to bring Eve into sin, as Eve did in turn to Adam. Their sin, the paragraph continues, was wilful and unforced and this all happened with God's permission and according to his purpose, for his own glory, in accordance with his wise and holy will – in line with the teaching of chapter 3 on God's decree.

The world-shattering consequences experienced by all humanity as a result of this first human sin are spelled out in the remainder of chapter 6. These consequences are listed under six headings, which should nevertheless not be taken entirely separately: they are mutually connected and together flow from Adam's fall.

Loss of Edenic privileges

When Adam and Eve ate from the forbidden tree, they 'fell from their original righteousness and communion with God' (paragraph 2). The account in Genesis does not expressly say this, but it is clear from what happened: they hid from God (Gen. 3:8). The loving, trusting fellowship that they had until that time enjoyed with God was utterly broken. And the righteousness with which they had been created and which underpinned and enabled that fellowship had been destroyed.

Death

As a result, and just as God had threatened, death came upon Adam and Eve. Physical death would come later, but they experienced spiritual death immediately: they were 'dead in sin and wholly defiled in all the faculties and parts of soul and body'. This becomes obvious as the narrative of Genesis follows the unhappy couple out of Eden into the wilderness beyond: from the murder of one son by another, Adam and Eve's world is now taken over by sin. Violence, deceit, sexual immorality, theft and wrongdoing of all kinds – above all, the worship of false gods – became normal in this fallen world. And all died, as the fifth chapter of Genesis so evocatively demonstrates: 'and he died ... and he died ... and he died'.

Guilt

With sin comes guilt (paragraph 3). Guilt is often thought of as just a feeling. Because of this, the answer is said today to lie in therapy: we are to deal with feelings of guilt by talking through the possible underlying causes. This is not the way in which the Confession – or, more importantly, the Bible – speaks of guilt. Guilt is objective: it is not a matter of feelings but of judicial condemnation by God.

Corruption

Alongside guilt came corruption. Adam and Eve were 'made after the image of God, in knowledge, righteousness, and true holiness', as chapter 4 of the Confession puts it. When they fell, that was all lost. The image of God in them was not totally destroyed, but it was seriously marred. Their knowledge – referring particularly to spiritual knowledge – was darkened; righteousness and holiness were taken away. They did not become as evil as they could have been, but every human faculty in them was corrupted. As a result, they were now 'the servants of sin' (paragraph 3).

Sin

Worn brakes on a car will prevent the vehicle from stopping as it ought. Corrupt code will impede a computer's performance. The corruption which came into Adam and Eve's souls when they sinned prevented them from living lives of righteousness, pleasing to God, and launched them upon a life of sin. Their original sin brought forth the fruit of more and more sins. Sin was now their way of life.

Miseries

With sin came misery. Eden had been a paradise: a place of holy, pure joy. Adam and Eve had been intensely, continuously happy – in one another, in the garden where they lived, in their work and supremely in God. Now they were cast out of Eden and they were miserable, living under the curse that God had declared upon the world. Eve experienced the pains of childbirth; Adam knew for the first time what it was to sweat and toil over his work – frustration took the place of fulfilment, weakness and failure came instead of strength and success, suffering beset them at every turn.

Eating from the forbidden tree was disastrous for Adam and Even. The focus of chapter 6 of the Confession, however, is to affirm that it was disastrous also for the whole of humanity. Each of the six consequences of their sin outlined above has also come upon us. This is an essential element in the structure of the theology taught by the Confession.

Chapter 6 makes clear that these consequences came upon humanity at the very time of the Fall itself. It is not, as many think, that we are each born into this world and then commit sin and so experience all these consequences. Rather, as the Confession puts it, 'Our first parents by this sin fell … and we in them' (paragraph 2). They, as our 'root' and 'by God's appointment, standing in the room and stead of all mankind', plunged us all into the same sad condition when they first sinned. Each of us consequently comes into this world already in a state of guilt and corruption, under the wrath of God and liable to all the miseries of a fallen world and ultimately death.

Several points are worth noting here. We are all physically descended from Adam and Eve – 'by ordinary generation', as chapter 6 puts it (paragraph 3). On the principle that the fruit cannot be better than the tree from which it came, it is not possible for us to be born pure, righteous and holy from a stock that is corrupt. That is one reason for our being born in a state of sin.

The second, and arguably more significant, reason is that our first parents were also specifically appointed by God as the representative of all humanity. Strictly speaking, it is Adam who was so appointed (Rom. 5:12–21), as questions 19 and 21 of the Baptist Catechism of the 1690s make clear.

Thus guilt as well as corruption is ours from the moment we come into existence. This is felt by many in the West to be unfair, but that is simply a result of the overly individualistic worldview of our society. Those who grow up in other parts of the world seem to have little difficulty accepting the biblical view of corporate guilt due to the actions of a representative.

Because of this original sin, corruption and guilt with which we are born, we go on to commit 'actual transgressions' (paragraph 4). Like the fallen Adam and Eve, every part of us is corrupt and prone to sin. We are not as bad as we could be, but equally there is nothing in us that can truly be called good. We are 'utterly indisposed, disabled, and made opposite to all good, and wholly inclined to all evil' (paragraph 4).

Society is convinced that humans are basically good. That is not true: we are, as fallen creatures, fundamentally evil. We are not good people who sometimes do bad things; we are bad people who continually do bad things. The things that we think, imagine and dream are sinful; our aims in life are ungodly and selfish; our hearts are wicked. We do not do wrong against our will; we want to disobey God and go our own way.

Many of our difficulties in life stem from an inadequate grasp of this biblical teaching on sin. Because we do not see how deeply sin has gripped the human race, we misunderstand what is needed to put it right and so fail to appreciate the biblical doctrine of salvation by grace alone. We do not see the gravity of our sin and so fail to understand why anyone should suffer for ever in hell for it. We do not see that our plight is so bad that only Christ can save us, so we underestimate what he has done for sinners and think that we can contribute something to our own salvation. We do not understand the terrible grip that sin has on our hearts and so fail to apply with trembling hearts to the Lord for help in temptation.

Some Christians believe that it is possible, as believers, to reach a state of perfection of some kind in this life. This unbiblical idea arises, again, from an inadequate grasp of the Bible's teaching about sin. The Confession rightly says: 'This corruption of nature, during this life, doth remain in those that are regenerated' (paragraph 5) and so sin continues to haunt us until we die. It is deeply ingrained and even its 'first motions' – the first appearance and sense of sin in the deepest recesses of our hearts – 'are truly and properly sin'.

It is for this reason that the Bible points us to the work of God alone, in Christ alone, for salvation – and the Confession follows suit. It introduces this grand subject next, in chapter 7, by addressing the topic of covenant.

Covenant (chapter 7)

A covenant, in biblical terms, is an arrangement initiated by God, in which he sets out the terms on which he will deal with an individual, a people or the entire human race. The theology of the covenants, particularly the precise nature of and relationship between those described in the Old Testament and the new covenant in Christ, was one of the few areas of real disagreement between the framers of the 1689 Confession and their paedobaptist brethren at the

Westminster Assembly. It is therefore no surprise that this chapter of the 1689 Confession departs significantly from the equivalent chapter of the Westminster Confession (and the congregationalist Savoy Declaration).

Furthermore, the 1689 Confession is the first major Baptist confession to address the subject of covenants in a theological manner: the 1644 First London Confession deals with the new covenant or covenant of grace (see especially Articles X, XII), but does not expressly expound how the various covenants referred to in Scripture relate to each other theologically.

Chapter 7 begins in the same way as the Westminster Confession and follows the Savoy Declaration even more closely. God is so far above humanity that we could never attain eternal life without 'some voluntary condescension on God's part'. This is so even before the fall; how much more so once man had fallen into sin (paragraph 2). And so all three confessions are at pains to make clear what the previous chapter has already established: there is no way that humanity could redeem itself from the terrible condition into which the sin of Adam has plunged it. Men and women were doomed, unless heaven intervened.

What was needed was 'some voluntary condescension of God's part' (paragraph 1), which is precisely what the Lord in his grace has provided, 'by way of covenant' – and because of sin, this must be a 'covenant of grace' (paragraph 2). A covenant of grace, which God 'freely offereth unto sinners', is the vehicle chosen by God for the communication to fallen humanity of the divine grace so desperately needed for redemption.

The next paragraph in the Westminster Confession deals with the covenant of works. This is omitted in the 1689 Confession, leading some to suggest that the particular Baptists of that time did not believe in such a covenant. This is untrue: the phrase 'covenant of works' is used expressly in chapters 19.6 and 20.1 of the 1689 Confession. In addition, the terms of the covenant of works are set out in chapter 6, paragraph 1, which speaks of the 'righteous law' that God gave to Adam at creation, 'which had been unto life had he kept it; and threatened death upon the breach thereof'. This is confirmed by the reference in paragraph 1 of chapter 7 to 'the reward of life'. In Question 15 of the Baptist Confession, it is called a 'covenant of life'. The 1689 Confession certainly teaches a covenant of works.

The covenant of works (or life) was, however, of no use to fallen humanity because sin made people utterly unable to keep God's righteous law. God showed his grace by making a covenant of grace. The following two paragraphs of chapter 7 explain, first, the substance of this covenant (paragraph 2) and then how it was revealed (paragraph 3). Under the covenant of grace, the Lord 'freely offereth unto sinners, life and salvation by Jesus Christ'. These are vital words (especially in the light of the Baptist hypercalvinist controversies of the eighteenth century). God's election, before the creation of the world, of certain individuals for salvation, and Christ's death to redeem those elect individuals in particular in no way cancels the genuineness of the free offer of the gospel.

The biblical balance is maintained in paragraph 2 by the juxtaposition of the need for faith in Christ in order to be saved ('requiring of them faith in him, that they may be saved') and the promise of the Spirit to the elect 'to make them willing and able to believe'. The twin truths of the need for the sinner to trust in Christ for salvation and his inability so to do without the prior work of the Holy Spirit are thus elegantly brought together.

The chapter finally (paragraph 3) sets out how this covenant of grace was made known to humanity. The covenant did not originate with Christ's incarnation. It is founded in an eternal, pre-temporal covenant between the Father and the Son 'about the redemption of the elect'. It is on the basis of this covenant of redemption that the covenant of grace was made. This latter covenant is 'revealed in the gospel; first of all to Adam', in Genesis 3:15; then 'by farther steps', referring to the covenants of the Old Testament (without naming them); finally, 'the full discovery thereof was completed in the New Testament' with the coming of Christ.

The restraint of the 1689 Confession at this point is remarkable, given that these brief phrases relate to an area of the greatest contention with paedobaptists. The Westminster Confession of Faith states the classic paedobaptist position that there was one covenant of grace 'differently administered' in the Old and New Testaments (WCF 7.5,6). On this construction, the various covenants of the Old Testament were in fact each a different manifestation, or administration, of the one covenant of grace.

The 1689 Confession agrees that there is only one covenant of grace and affirms that this covenant was 'revealed ... in farther steps' as the Old Testament progressed. It was, however, as the Baptists understood it, 'completed' only with the coming of Christ in the New Testament. The Old Testament covenants were thus preparatory to the full establishment of the new covenant in Christ.

The final statement of the chapter underlines two truths, one positive and one negative. Negatively, fallen humanity is 'now utterly incapable of acceptance with God upon those terms, on which Adam stood in his state of innocency'; in other words, the covenant of works is of no use to us in our fallen condition. We cannot save ourselves, nor can we in any way contribute to our salvation.

Positively, and only by the covenant of grace, sinners may be saved and obtain 'life and a blessed immortality'. The manner in which this was made possible by the work of Christ the mediator and how this work is brought to and made effective in the lives and experience of sinners are the topics of the chapters that follow.

> Let Satan and the world
> now rage or now allure;
> the promises in Christ are made
> immutable and sure.
>
> The oath infallible
> is now my spirit's trust;
> I know that He who spoke the word
> is faithful, true and just.
>
> William Williams and C.H. Spurgeon

Study questions

1. Reflect on how the Bible's teaching on the fall of humanity in Adam helps us understand the state of our world today.

2. Ponder what this teaching means for your own condition, before and after conversion to Christ.

3. What comforts does the new covenant in Christ bring to the believer?

Further reading

Thomas Boston, *Human Nature in Its Fourfold State* (repr., Edinburgh: Banner of Truth, 1964), Sections I, II

Samuel D. Renihan, *The Mystery of Christ: His Covenant & His Kingdom* (Cape Coral, FL: Founders Press, 2019)

Pascal Denault, *The Distinctiveness of Baptist Covenant Theology: A Comparison Between Seventeenth-Century Particular Baptist and Paedobaptist Federalism*, trans. M. & E. Wigfield (Solid Ground, 2013)

Chapter 8:
Christ the Mediator

Chapter 8 of the 1689 Confession, headed 'Of Christ the Mediator', is an exquisite summary of scriptural teaching on the person of our Saviour and his work of redemption. It is beautifully concise, biblically faithful, theologically sound and historically consistent. It provides a vital, eternal perspective on the work of salvation.

Our tendency is to think of salvation in terms of what it does for us – regeneration, justification, sanctification, glorification, and so on. The Confession wants us to start a long way further back – in eternity. That is why it began its exposition of salvation, in chapter 7, with the covenant and especially the covenant of redemption made in eternity past within the counsel of the trinitarian God himself (referred to also in chapter 8, paragraph 1). If chapter 7 of the Confession gives us the covenantal outline of God's plan of salvation, chapter 8 enables us to see the manner in which that plan has been fulfilled in and through the person and work of Christ the mediator.

This pivotal chapter in the Confession's exposition of salvation may be examined by means of three questions: who carried out the work of salvation; how did he do this; and what was the outcome?

Who carried out the work of salvation?

Who could possibly be properly qualified to carry out the great work of the redemption of sinners? Chapter 8 of the Confession answers this question: it is the Lord Jesus Christ. He alone is the one who is qualified to be the mediator between God and man under the eternal covenant of redemption. He it is whom God has appointed to be 'the Prophet, Priest and King; Head and Saviour of his Church, the heir of all things, and judge of the world'.

What is it that qualified Christ for this work? It is the fact that God appointed him to it: 'It pleased God in his eternal purpose, to choose and ordain the Lord Jesus ... to be the Mediator between God and man' (paragraph 1). What more do we need? Here is God's appointed workman for the epic work that he planned in eternity, the redemption of humanity.

Firstly, he is truly and fully God. He is God's 'only begotten Son' (paragraph 1), 'the second person in the Holy Trinity' (paragraph 2). He is the 'Son of God' who is 'very and eternal God, the brightness of the Father's glory, of one substance and equal with him', the creator, sustainer and governor of all things (paragraph 2).

The Confession could not be clearer: Jesus Christ is in every sense God; he is not an angel; he is not some kind of secondary or subsidiary God; he is not simply endowed by God with some kind of divine nature, or given divine titles. He is God. Who better to be mediator between God and man? Who else could be suited for the work of redemption?

Amazingly, however, that is not enough. As the Confession goes on to affirm, secondly, the mediator who is God took to himself a human nature in order to be qualified for the work of redemption. At the right time, he 'did ... take unto him man's nature, with all the essential properties, and common infirmities thereof, yet without sin' (paragraph 2). This was achieved through the virginal conception of the young Israelite woman Mary, by the power of the Holy Spirit, with the result that Christ was 'made of a woman, of the tribe of Judah, of the seed of Abraham, and David according to the Scriptures' (paragraph 2).

In other words, it was a true and complete human nature that Christ took to himself in the incarnation. Unlike our fallen nature, this human nature of Christ's was sinless. This did not make Christ's humanity any less human: being sinful by nature is not an essential part of being human. We have to say, as theologians over the centuries have generally concluded, that our redemption could not have been accomplished without this incarnation: that the mediator between God and man had to be truly human as well as fully God. This is what the Lord Jesus is. He is a fully qualified, perfectly suited mediator for the work of redemption (1 Tim. 2:5).

The mediator is thus one person (the Lord Jesus, the eternal Son of God) with two natures (divine and human), as chapter 8 states expressly at the end of its second paragraph: 'So that two whole, perfect and distinct natures were inseparably joined together in one person'. The divine and human natures of Christ are united in his one person in such a manner that the resulting union can never be undone ('inseparably joined').

The phrases that follow this statement are crucial: 'without conversion, composition or confusion' – in other words, the divine and human natures of Christ are clearly distinguishable as divine and human and have not been subject to change of any kind, nor has one nature been absorbed or obliterated by the other (no 'conversion'); and the two natures are in no way mixed or confused with each other (no 'composition or confusion'), so as to produce some kind of third nature that would be neither truly divine nor truly human. Christ is truly one person with two natures.

This is so, even though Scripture occasionally says of one nature that which is, strictly speaking, true of the other nature (for example, that the church 'of God' was 'purchased with his own blood', Acts 20:28 – see paragraph 7 of chapter 8). These truths are absolutely vital and fundamental to our salvation. If Christ were anything other than what these words of the Confession specify, he would not be suitably qualified as mediator between God and man. We would then have no hope of salvation.

It took the church a long time in the early centuries of the gospel age to come clearly to the conclusion that this was indeed the teaching of Scripture and to formulate language that would properly reflect this teaching. There were sharp, prolonged disputes over, first, whether Christ was truly and fully God and then whether he was truly and fully human and, finally, how precisely the two natures – divine and human – related to one another and to the one person of the incarnate Christ.

The teaching about the person of Christ that emerged from these disputes was encapsulated in the creeds and confessions that have come down to us over the centuries – in particularly, the Nicene creed in the form finally adopted at the Council of

Constantinople in AD 381 and the definition agreed at the Council of Chalcedon in AD 451. It is this teaching that is encapsulated in chapter 8 of our Confession (and in the equivalent sections of other reformed confessions).

The closeness of the wording of the 1689 Confession on this point with that of the Westminster Confession and the Savoy Declaration underlines the unity of Christian teaching on this essential topic. At the same time, those who framed the 1689 Confession wished to preserve some of the wording from earlier confessions of faith with which they felt some affinity – in particular, the Separatists' True Confession of 1596 and the First London Baptist Confession of Faith of 1644.

Consequently, phrases from those confessions were included in chapter 8 of the 1689 Confession, notably in its paragraph 2 on the divine nature of Christ and his incarnation and in the closing two paragraphs – 9 and 10 – of chapter 8. Paragraph 9 asserts the uniqueness of Christ for this role: no one else could undertake it. The wording is from Article 12 of the True Confession, which appears also in Article 13 of the 1644 Confession. Then paragraph 10, the final paragraph of the Chapter, explains why we need a mediator who is prophet, priest and king: we need a prophet because of our ignorance, a priest because of our alienation from God and a king to rule, rescue and preserve us. The wording here is drawn from Article 14 of the 1644 Confession. These two paragraphs form a valuable addition to the chapter on the person of Christ, showing appropriate respect to those who framed former confessions of faith in the separatist and Baptist traditions.

What precisely is the nature of the work which Christ was appointed to accomplish? This is indicated at the end of the first paragraph of chapter 8. It is there summarised in terms of redemption, calling, justification, sanctification and glorification. In other words, the entire scope of salvation is encompassed in the work to which the Lord Jesus was called by the Father and which Christ accomplished as the incarnate Son.

The various aspects of the work of salvation will be the subject of the chapters of the Confession that follow, as they describe in more depth all that our mediator has accomplished for us. Yet there is one further aspect of this work highlighted by this first paragraph of chapter 8. That is the question, for whom was this work performed? Was it done for every human being who would ever live? The answer of the Confession is clear: the mediator's work was to be carried out for 'a people' who were given to Christ 'from all eternity ... to be his seed and to be by him in time redeemed, called, justified, sanctified and glorified'.

Christ was to redeem the elect (as they are described in chapter 3 of the Confession). This teaching – that the redemptive work of Christ was for the elect and not for every human being – so clearly stated here and in all the reformed confessions of this period was the commonly accepted doctrine of the reformed churches then, as it should be today.

How did the mediator carry out his work?

It is one thing to be qualified to perform some particular work; it is another thing actually to carry it out to completion. Chapter 8 has so far shown that the Lord Jesus is perfectly qualified to be the mediator between God and man. It now goes on to demonstrate how he carried out that work as the incarnate Son of God.

I wonder how you or I might begin to explain this, if it were left to us? I suspect that we might focus immediately on his life of perfect obedience and his death on our behalf as our sacrifice for sin. Chapter 8 deals with this, but it begins with an element in the saving work of Christ which we too often forget. Paragraph 3 tells how Christ was anointed by the Holy Spirit, so that 'he might be thoroughly furnished to execute the office of a mediator'.

What these words tell us is that the work of the Spirit in anointing and sanctifying (setting apart to the Father) the Lord Jesus was essential to Christ's work as mediator. This is entirely in line with the thrust of the biblical testimony which, in both Old and New Testaments, highlights the work of the Spirit in the ministry which the Messiah came to perform. The work of salvation is the work of the triune God.

This third paragraph of chapter 8 emphasises how fully the Lord Jesus Christ was equipped for his earthly ministry: he was 'anointed with the Holy Spirit, above measure'; 'all the treasure of wisdom and knowledge' were in him and 'all fullness' dwelt in him; he was 'holy, harmless, undefiled, and full of grace and truth'. He was thus 'thoroughly furnished to execute the office of a mediator and surety', having been called to that work by the Father (as we have seen in paragraph 1, above), 'who also put all power and judgement in his hand, and gave him commandment to execute the same'.

All of this is of the greatest comfort to the believer. Our mediator was perfectly equipped to accomplish the work of saving us, fully and perfectly. He lacked no power, skill, ability or competence for this great task. He never found himself short of precisely what he needed for his work. He was able, therefore, to complete it perfectly and in full.

This he did willingly, as paragraph 4 explains, and at tremendous personal cost. This involved: his perfectly fulfilling the law, without sin of any kind; taking 'the punishment due to us ..., being made sin and a curse for us'; and undergoing terrible suffering both of soul and of body. This all culminated in his agonising death by crucifixion and his burial. Gloriously, it was followed by his resurrection from the dead on the third day, 'with the same body in which he suffered'; his ascension into heaven, where he 'sitteth at the right hand of his Father' and makes intercession; and from where he 'shall return to judge men and angels, at the end of the world'.

This is the work of redemption! This is the work to which God the Father called his Son as mediator to perform; and this is the work that Jesus Christ completed perfectly, with nothing done inadequately and nothing left unfinished.

What did his work achieve?

Finally, chapter 8 tells us what the mediator's work accomplished. Paragraph 5 states that 'by his perfect obedience and sacrifice of himself, which he through the eternal Spirit once offered up unto God', Jesus did three things.

1. He 'fully satisfied the justice of God'. What a comfort that is! Note the word 'fully' – for the elect, there is no aspect of God's justice that is still to be satisfied, no element of punishment that has not been already borne on our behalf, no drop of divine wrath remaining in the cup to be drunk. All is satisfied!

2. Christ by his work of salvation 'procured reconciliation'. This is the central work of a mediator, to reconcile two parties. In

the case of the elect, it is God who had to be reconciled to sinful humanity, alienated from him by their sin. This work too has been perfectly accomplished. Whereas once we were children of wrath, without hope and God in this world, now by the blood of Christ we have been brought near (Eph. 2:3, 12, 13).

3. Christ's work of mediation has 'purchased an everlasting inheritance in the kingdom of heaven' for all the elect. Not only are we justified and reconciled, but we have been granted the inestimable riches of heaven for ever! All this is the work of Christ 'for all those whom the Father hath given unto him', without any contribution, work or merit of any kind on our part whatsoever. This is grace indeed.

How is the benefit of Christ's mediatorial work made ours?

The final question that arises concerns the application of this work to the elect. The answer is given in two parts.

1. How did it come to those who lived before Christ's earthly ministry? Chapter 8 makes clear that the work itself was not accomplished and 'the price of redemption was not actually paid' until Christ had completed that ministry (paragraph 6). Nevertheless, all the benefits of that work 'were communicated to the elect in all ages', even from the beginning of the world. In the Old Testament era, this happened through 'those promises, types and sacrifices, wherein he was revealed and signified to be the seed of

the woman, which should bruise the serpent's head; and the Lamb slain from the foundation of the world'. The elect of the Old Testament did not miss out on the benefits of Christ's work, even though they perceived them by faith only through types and shadows.

2. We who live in the gospel age, by contrast, receive the same blessings after the event, as it were, in the light of, rather than simply looking forward to, the incarnation, suffering, death and resurrection of our Saviour.

Whether we live before or after the earthly ministry of Christ, we have the redemption won for us by Christ applied to us in the same way, as paragraph 8 of chapter 8 asserts: Christ intercedes for us, unites us to himself by the Spirit, reveals the mystery of salvation to us through his word, persuades us to believe and obey, governs our hearts by his word and Spirit and overcomes all our enemies by his power and wisdom.

All this, says paragraph 8, is entirely consistent with 'his wonderful, and unsearchable dispensation' and it is 'all of free, and absolute grace, without any condition foreseen in them [i.e. the elect] to procure it'. In other words, salvation is completely free to us: there is nothing that we are to, or can, do. It is in every respect accomplished, guaranteed and underwritten (this is the meaning of the reference in paragraph 3 to Christ's being our 'surety') for us by Christ.

Christ is the mediator appointed by God to reconcile God and man according to the eternal covenant of redemption; and he has accomplished the work committed to him perfectly and completely,

for the benefit of all whom the Father has given him. To him be all
the praise and all the glory!

> Glory, glory everlasting
>> be to him who bore the cross!
> who redeemed our souls, by tasting
>> death, the death deserved by us:
>>> spread His glory,
>> who redeemed His people thus.

Thomas Kelly

Study questions

1. Look up the verses in the New Testament that refer to Christ as
mediator. What is the function of a mediator and why do we need
one? Why is Christ the only one who is suitable to be the mediator
between God and humanity?

2. Think about what paragraph 2 affirms. Why is it essential for our
salvation that Christ have both a divine and a human nature? And
that he is one person only? Why would salvation fail if our saviour
were (a) not divine, (b) not human, (c) not a single person?

3. Identify the stages of the human life lived by Christ, as described
in this chapter, and the various events to which the chapter refers.
How do these confirm your faith in Christ as mediator and your
assurance of salvation through his work?

4. Consider the teaching of chapter 8 on the work of Christ as our
prophet, priest and king. What do these each teach us about what
Christ has done, is doing and will do for his people?

Further reading

Donald Macleod, *The Person of Christ* (Leicester: Inter-Varsity Press, 1998)

John Owen, *The Glory of Christ*, abridged by R. J. K. Law (Edinburgh: Banner of Truth, 1994)

D. M. Lloyd-Jones, *The Cross: God's Way of Salvation* (Kingsway, 1986)

Chapter 9:
Free Will

From time to time, I am asked whether I believe in free will. If everything happens just as God decrees, what room is there left for human free will? I suspect that I am expected to respond with an outright denial of free will – and no doubt protests and objections to my outlandish opinion will duly follow. For that reason, I often begin by answering their question in the positive – a response that is in sympathy with this chapter of the 1689 Confession, which is entitled 'Of Free Will'.

Free will is a subject both of controversy and of confusion among Christians. Any suggestion that we do not have free will can be met with horror, incredulity or straightforward contradiction. When we affirm from Scripture the sovereignty of God in all things, it is retorted that humans cannot then be held responsible for their sin. When we argue from the Bible, as we must, that humans do not enjoy unconstrained freedom of will in every sense, it is often assumed that we must therefore be saying that we are mere robots, with no will of our own of any kind. This illustrates the confusion that surrounds this subject in many people's minds.

Confusion on this topic is, however, unsurprising. The human will and its relationship to God's sovereignty ultimately exceed the bounds of what we are able to grasp. That is why we must ensure that we pay very close attention to what the Bible teaches in these areas and seek to hold to it all, not merely to just one aspect or another. It is here that the 1689 Confession is so helpful, as, in chapter 9, it states the scriptural position fully, clearly and precisely, making the necessary, careful distinctions that we find in the biblical teaching on the subject. Chapter 9 follows the equivalent chapters of the Westminster Confession of Faith and of the Savoy Declaration of Faith and Order almost word for word. On this topic, the reformed confessions speak with one voice.

The 1689 Confession first makes a general statement about the human will (paragraph 1) and then describes the four different states of the will which correspond to the four different spiritual states in which a person may be found (paragraphs 2 to 5).

Liberty of choice (paragraph 1)

Do humans enjoy freedom of will? Yes, says the Confession in the opening paragraph of chapter 9. It affirms that God has 'indued the will of man' with 'natural liberty, and power of acting upon choice'. The statement is qualified to make clear the kind of 'natural liberty' that the human will enjoys: it is a liberty of choice that is 'neither forced, nor by any necessity of nature determined to do good or evil'. Three texts of Scripture are cited to justify these statements: Matthew 17:12, where the Lord Jesus Christ speaks of how they 'did whatever they pleased to him' to Elijah (that is, John the Baptist); James 1:14, which speaks of temptation in terms of our 'own evil desire'; and Deuteronomy 30:19, where Moses sets before the people of Israel 'life and death, blessing and curse' and calls on them to 'choose life'. These three verses demonstrate that Scripture speaks of humans making choices and deciding as they please.

So humans have a liberty – a freedom – to choose, as well as a power to act on the choices that we make. This liberty is real. We can and do decide and choose all the time what we want and we act on those decisions and choices. We are not robots. The Confession brings this teaching out in the second half of paragraph 1: our wills are 'not forced' (reflecting the language of chapter 3, paragraph 1, 'nor is violence offered to the will of the creature'), nor are our wills 'determined', either for good or evil, 'by any necessity of nature'. There is nothing external to the human person that compels their will to decide in a certain way. In particular, God does not force, override or coerce our wills. There is also nothing naturally inherent in our make-up or in the constitution of reality which means that our wills are determined in some way and are not free to act as we choose. The choices that we make are genuinely ours; the decisions that we take are truly our decisions. We might, then, say that we do indeed have 'free will', though in the light of the full teaching of Scripture that is summarised in this chapter, it would be better to speak in terms of our having 'free agency' – the phrase traditionally used for this purpose, to reflect the constraints upon us and within us that are noted in what follows.

For we need to be clear about what precisely is meant by these statements. It is obvious that what we want and what we get are often different things. I may at this moment want to enjoy a piece of chocolate cake, but I may not be able to fulfil that desire because there is none available to me at present. That is not a denial of my liberty of choice. It is, rather, a limitation imposed by my circumstances. More seriously, if someone were to enter my study as I write this and brandish a revolver at me, threatening to shoot me if I did not hand over my wallet, I would no doubt give them my wallet even though I would not, ideally, want to do so. I am constrained by circumstances, not by any restriction on the liberty of my will, strictly speaking. Faced with the choice of handing over my wallet and being shot, I freely choose the former.

It is this liberty of choice that underpins human responsibility for our actions and decisions. It is because of this that God is justified in punishing us for our sin, as our sin represents the exercise of our own choice to disobey God. This is so, notwithstanding God's sovereignty over all things, including even our sinful actions (as affirmed by the Confession, chapter 5, paragraph 4, and chapter 6, paragraph 1). We cannot understand fully how God is absolutely sovereign and humans are responsible for their sin, but this is the clear teaching of Scripture and it is not an inherently self-contradictory position. Our sin is our responsibility, not God's – we cannot blame him for it and he is justified in holding us accountable for it.

There is, however, more to be said on the subject of the human will. The Bible teaches that the state of our wills varies according to our spiritual condition. It will be seen that the differences relate to the ability of our wills to choose what is spiritually good and pleasing to God. The Confession is not interested in whether I choose to put jam or honey on my bread for tea. It is very interested in whether I choose to obey God or decide instead to sin against him. This is reflected in the following paragraphs of this chapter, which address the question in relation to the fourfold state of humanity.

Innocence (paragraph 2)

As created, in 'his state of innocency', Adam was free to choose 'that which was good, and well-pleasing to God'. He also had the power to carry out that choice. There was no impediment of any kind on the human will, to inhibit a person from deciding to obey God. The text cited for this is Ecclesiastes 7:29, which affirms that 'God made people upright'. (We could cite here, in addition, Gen. 1:26, 31; 1 Tim. 2:13–14.)

Yet we know that Adam and Eve did not obey God in the end: they broke the law given to them, to the effect that they were not to eat of the tree of the knowledge of good and evil. The Confession recognises this by stating that the human will in Eden was 'mutable', or changeable, with the result that humanity 'might fall from' the state of innocence (citing Genesis 3:6). This reflects what the Confession has already stated, that Adam and Eve were created with the 'possibility of transgressing, being left to the liberty of their own will, which was subject to change' (chapter 4, paragraph 2). Our first parents were, in their original state, free to obey God, but were also free to disobey him if they so choose. And, tragically, they did so choose.

Fall (paragraph 3)

No reader of the Bible who pays attention to the story-line of Scripture can fail to notice the enormous change that occurs as

Adam and Eve are cast out of Eden at the end of the third chapter of Genesis. Of greatest significance is the fact that, after that tragic event, humans (with just one exception) sin – consistently and universally. Beginning with Cain's murder of his brother Abel, the human story is one of constant disobedience to God. And just as all sinned, so all died, as Genesis 5 underlines with its refrain, 'then he died'.

Paul takes up the theme in his letter to the Romans when he affirms that, because of Adam's sin, all have sinned (Rom. 5:12 – see also 3:23). In doing so, the apostle is only reflecting the words that fell from the Lord's lips in response to one who addressed him as 'good teacher': 'No one is good except God alone' (Mk. 10:18). Every human (except Jesus Christ) is a sinner and sins. What does this have to say about the state of our wills?

The Confession is very clear: in our fallen state, we have 'wholly lost all ability of will, to any spiritual good accompanying salvation'. It is worth noting the qualification in this statement. Fallen humanity has not lost all ability to make free choices. The Confession makes no suggestion here that our freedom to sin has been curtailed. Nor, indeed, does it say that we have no desire ever to do anything even relatively good. Its affirmation of the loss that our wills have suffered relates only to 'any spiritual good accompanying salvation'. We do not have the ability to will to do anything that might help us to be saved.

Our wills are not what they were in Eden, where we delighted to please God. They are now impaired, damaged. As Paul puts it, quoting the psalms, 'There is no one righteous, not even one ... All have turned away ... For all have sinned' (Rom. 3:10, 12, 23). This state of affairs is the outworking of the corruption that entered into every part of humanity at the fall (as the Confession has already affirmed, in chapter 6, paragraphs 2 and 4). So we are, the Confession continues, 'altogether averse from that good and dead in sin' and so each one is unable in his own strength 'to convert himself; or to prepare himself thereunto'. We have no desire to trust in Christ or to repent of sin or to seek refuge in the Saviour. There is absolutely nothing in our wills, as fallen creatures, which inclines us in that direction at all.

We need to be clear at this point that our wills are a part of us – they do not sit outside us somewhere, dictating and restricting what we would really, in ourselves, like to do. The human person is a unity – so our wills form part of our make-up: they reflect our beliefs, values, desires, character and personality. Our wills are not independent of us, nor random. We have no desires deep down within us, which some restriction or constraint on our wills is preventing us from expressing. Our will is ours – it is the expression of what we truly want, a perfect reflection of our genuine desires.

So when the Confession, in line with Scripture, says that we have no ability to will any spiritual good, it means that we have no desire of any kind for such good. We are, as it says, 'averse' from it. When Adam fell, humanity lost all appetite for true spiritual good. That is why Jesus said, 'No one can come to me unless the Father who sent him draws him' (Jn. 6:44). It is not that God has put some obstacle in the way of someone who otherwise desperately wants to come to him. No – we have no desire, no will of any kind, to come to God, unless he draws us. In our fallen state, we are, as another of the verses cited by this paragraph affirms, 'enslaved by various passions and pleasures' (Tit. 3:3) – captive to our own sinful desires, willing only to go on in our sin.

Salvation (paragraph 4)

All this changes when 'God converts a sinner and translates him into the state of grace'. Notice that the Confession rightly attributes our conversion to God – it has to be God who converts, for, as we have already seen, we have no desire or will of our own to be saved. At the point of conversion, says the Confession, God frees the sinner from 'natural bondage under sin' and 'by his grace alone, enables him freely to will, and to do that which is spiritually good'. As Paul puts it, 'although you used to be slaves of sin, you obeyed from the heart that pattern of teaching to which you were handed over, and having been set free from sin, you became enslaved to righteousness' (Rom. 6:17–18).

This is tremendous news. As one whom God has set free at conversion, the believer is now able to will to do what is good and pleasing to God. The Confession sounds a note of caution, however: we cannot yet do this perfectly, because of 'remaining corruptions'; indeed, we still 'also will that which is evil'. Our wills now are freed, yet not wholly. While we can and do true spiritual good, that good is imperfect; and we also continue willingly to do what is sinful. We are not yet perfect.

It is important that we affirm both aspects of the biblical truth here confessed. Christians tend (as ever) to go to one of two extremes here. Some want to affirm that believers are able to live without sin, or nearly so. And we are all prone to believe that we are better than we in fact are. We underestimate our sin; we do not see the full extent to which we still fall short of God's glory. We need then to be reminded of the qualification in this paragraph of the Confession – that we are not perfect and we still will what is evil.

This aspect of the Confession's teaching simply reflects what Paul tells us of his own experience as a believer in Romans 7.

Others, however, may be so conscious of continuing sinfulness as to be uneasy with any affirmation that the believer can do anything good at all. We so emphasise the ongoing corruption inherent in all our choices and acts that we will not admit that they ever should be called 'good' in any sense. Yet Paul affirms, in the text cited by the Confession at this point, that God works in us to will and to do his good pleasure (Phil. 2:13). And in his letter to the Ephesians, Paul writes of how the believer is 'created in Christ Jesus for good works, which God prepared in advance for us to do' (Eph. 2:10). We can, as believers, by faith, please God, although not perfectly so. We must hold on to both aspects of this vital truth, so as to have a balanced, biblical view of the realities of the Christian life.

Glory (paragraph 5)

Yet things will not always be this way, for the believer. The final paragraph of this vital chapter of the Confession is very short but makes a wonderful affirmation: 'The will of man is made perfectly, and immutably free to good alone, in the state of glory only'. Three things need to be briefly underlined here.

1. In glory the believer's will is changed so that it will be 'perfectly' free to 'good alone'. Unlike the state of the converted in this life, where the will is imperfectly inclined to good and may will evil, all corruption and imperfection will be removed in glory and the only thing that we will want, totally and uninterruptedly, is that which is perfectly holy and good.

2. This state cannot be changed – the will is made 'immutably' free to good alone, in a manner that is utterly irreversible. This contrasts sharply with the state of innocence, in Eden, where the will was not impeded from willing perfect good, but was changeable – and change it did. In glory, that will not be the case: the will of the believer will be unchangeable and perfectly inclined for ever to what is truly good. In the words of Hebrews 12:23, we will be numbered among the 'spirits of righteous people made perfect'.

3. It is only in glory that this will be the case – we cannot hope to achieve that perfect state before that time. We can, however, look forward with full confidence to our entry into glory, when, in the words of the verse cited by the Confession at this point, we will 'all reach unity in the faith and in the knowledge of God's Son, growing into maturity with a stature measured by Christ's fullness' (Eph. 4:13).

Conclusion

The four states of humanity described above have helpfully been summarised in this way:

- in the state of innocence, man was able to sin or not to sin;
- in his fallen state, man is not able not to sin;
- in his regenerate state, a believer is able not to sin;
- in his glorified state, the believer is not able to sin.

And so the believer can sing with confidence about the life to come:

Then we shall be where we would be,

then we shall be what we should be,

that which is not now, nor could be,

    then shall be our own.

Thomas Kelly

Study questions

1. If we are incapable of any spiritual good before we come to faith in Christ, what does this mean for the work of preaching and evangelism? (See Acts 2:37; 4:12; 16:14, 30–31.)

2. Think about the role of the Holy Spirit in relation to the believer's will, to conform it to the will of Christ. (See Phil. 2:13 and Eph. 4:17 – 6:9.)

3. What does the teaching of paragraph 5 of this chapter, on the state of the believer's will in glory, mean in practice, do you think? Consider Colossians 3:12–17 and the descriptions of heaven in the book of Revelation.

Further reading

Thomas Boston, *Human Nature in Its Fourfold State* (repr., Edinburgh: Banner of Truth, 1964)

Martin Luther, *The Bondage of the Will*, trans. J. I. Packer & O. R. Johnston (repr., Baker, 2012)

Chapter 10:
Effectual Calling

How is it that anyone ever comes to saving faith in Christ? That is the question that we should be asking, if we have understood the teaching of the 1689 Confession so far on the spiritual condition of fallen humanity. Chapters 6 and 9, in particular, have painted a desperate picture. We have learned in chapter 6 that we are 'dead in sin and wholly defiled, in all the faculties and parts of soul and body'; that Adam's guilt is imputed and his corrupt nature conveyed to every one of us; that we are therefore 'conceived in sin ... children of wrath, servants of sin and the subjects of death and all other miseries'; and that, as a result, we are 'utterly indisposed, disabled and made opposite to all good and wholly inclined to evil'.

To put the matter beyond doubt, chapter 9 has then taught us that the fallen human has 'wholly lost all ability of will, to any spiritual good accompanying salvation' and 'is not able, by his own strength, to convert himself' or even 'to prepare himself thereunto'. It makes no sense, then, to suggest that fallen men or women can or will, of themselves, take any step at all towards saving repentance and faith in Christ. So how can anyone ever be saved? Chapter 10 provides the answer.

The effectual call: what it is (paragraph 1)

Chapter 10 of the Confession teaches that a sinner is converted to Christ only when God effectually calls him or her. The Bible tells us of two kinds of call issued to sinners. There is the general call, which goes to everyone without discrimination. An illustration of this is given by the Lord in the parable of the sower (Mt. 13:18–23), in which the seed is sown indiscriminately and falls on various kinds of soil, some receptive and some not. So the message of the gospel is proclaimed to all, but not all who hear respond with saving faith: 'Many are invited, but few are chosen' (Mt. 22:14).

There is, then, a second kind of call, with which chapter 10 is concerned. This is the 'calling' that Paul refers to in Romans 8:30. It is an 'effectual', or as we would say today, 'effective', calling because all those to whom it is addressed come to Christ and are saved. There are no exceptions to this; the golden chain that Paul describes in that verse, running from election in eternity past to glory in eternity future, can never be broken. Every one of the elect is, in God's time, effectually called and that call is effective to bring them 'out of that state of sin and death, in which they are by nature, to grace and salvation by Jesus Christ'.

Effectual calling is, then, the crucial point at which God's work of salvation enters into the life and experience of the elect sinner. From the sinner's viewpoint, this is the moment at which he is born again – it is his regeneration. He is brought to true repentance; at this time, he is justified, adopted and set apart to God and the lifelong work of sanctification begins in him. This is the experience that we often call 'conversion' and which turns the life of the sinner around, so that he no longer serves himself and sin, but begins to serve Christ, from a regenerate heart and a conscience purged of the guilt of sin. It is the defining moment in the sinner's life on this earth.

How and when does this happen in a sinner's experience? The opening paragraph of chapter 10 addresses first the question of time: God acts in this way on an elect sinner 'in his [God's] appointed and accepted time'. How does this occur? Such a change in a fallen sinner requires a work of immense depth, extent and power, such as only God himself can perform. The effectual call therefore, as chapter 10 explains, impacts the mind, the heart and the will of the elect sinner; it penetrates to the very depths of the sinner's being and to every part of that being. And to bring this about, God uses 'his word and Spirit'.

This is of tremendous importance and is dealt with in more depth in chapter 20 of the Confession. At this point, we simply need to note the connection that Paul makes (Rom. 10:14–17) between faith and the hearing of the gospel. People come to faith – the call comes to them effectually – as a result of the proclamation and the hearing of the good news of Christ. This may be formally, for example at a service where the gospel is preached, or informally, for example through the testimony of a friend or by reading a tract, but one way or another, God's word must come to the sinner. Then, as the word comes, the Holy Spirit works in that sinner, to cause him to respond savingly to the message which they have heard. It is by these means – word and Spirit, working together – that God effectually calls elect sinners to salvation.

Let us turn now to the sinner: what effect do word and Spirit have, in order to make the call that comes to them effective? The Confession notes three effects.

1. The mind is enlightened, 'spiritually, and savingly to understand the things of God'. This is a reminder of our spiritual blindness by nature. Without the work of the Spirit to open the eyes of our understanding (Acts 26:18; Eph. 1:18), we remain utterly incapable of grasping or believing spiritual truths.

2. God removes the sinner's heart of stone and replaces it with a 'heart of flesh' (Ezek. 36:26). The heart, in biblical terms, is the centre of the personality – that which gives motive, drive and direction to life. The sinner is born with a heart of stone and so is dead in sin; a heart transplant is needed, which only the Spirit of God can perform. This is part of the divine work of effectual calling, giving a responsive and living heart in place of the sinner's cold, dead one.

3. The will is renewed: the sinner's wishes, desires, plans and objectives are radically altered, so that what is now desired is spiritual life and good. Above all, a person wishes to know Christ.

It should be underlined that these three elements of the work of the effectual call – on mind, heart and will – happen all together; they are not sequential, but rather different aspects of the same work.

The effect of this work is tremendous: it is described in the first paragraph of chapter 10 as 'effectually drawing them [sinners] to

Jesus Christ'. In that simple phrase we have the whole of salvation. And, as this paragraph makes clear, the sinner so drawn comes to Christ 'most freely, being made willing by [God's] grace'.

One of the great objections made against the doctrine of effectual calling is that it may sound as if God forces the sinner to believe on Christ. Nothing could be further from the truth. No compulsion is involved; God does not treat us as robots; he does not override our wills. Rather, he works by his mysterious, sovereign power on our very wills themselves, to woo them and change them, so that we will – freely, as the Confession states – come to Christ. As a result of God's work of effectual calling, the sinner wants nothing more than to trust in Christ. Christ is his delight, his love, his all.

The effectual call: its basis (paragraph 2)

The framers of the 1689 Confession were at pains to underline that the work of effectual calling is all of the grace and power of God – there is no contribution from the sinner. To this end, the second paragraph of chapter 10 states that the effectual call does not result from 'any thing at all foreseen in man'. This answers the Arminian claim that God elects on the basis of his foreknowledge: that he knows the future and so is able to see in advance which individuals will in fact come to saving faith in Christ. Paragraph 2 denies that God effectually calls particular individuals on this basis, or on any basis at all related to what God foresees in someone. Effectual calling has nothing to do with the character, beliefs, actions, experience or anything at all in or related to the individuals called. The effectual call 'is of God's free and special grace alone'.

The paragraph goes on to make clear that there is also no question of any co-operation between a person and God in the work of effectual calling. Just as effectual calling is not founded in anything that God foresees in the individual, neither does it involve any human contribution of any kind. It is not 'from any power or agency in the creature', co-working with his special grace. In fact, the individual to whom the effectual call comes is 'wholly passive therein', being 'dead in sins and trespasses'.

The voice of God that brings life comes to dead people (Jn. 5:25; Eph. 2:5) who by definition are able to do nothing at all. This doctrine, so clearly taught in the Scriptures, entirely removes from humans any ground for pride or self-congratulation in salvation. They have contributed nothing; all is of God. All the glory for redemption, therefore, goes to God.

This does not mean, however, that the one who is effectually called remains inactive. The whole point of this call is to create new life in him. When the call comes to a person, they are 'quickened and renewed by the Holy Spirit' and so 'enabled to answer this call, and to embrace the grace offered and conveyed in it'. As we saw in paragraph 1, the effectual call involves the enlightening of the mind, the enlivening of the heart and the renewal of the will. This is the same experience, described in different terms, as the quickening and renewing by the Holy Spirit of paragraph 2. Notice how even though this work is of the entire Godhead, in the Confession, as in Scripture, it is particularly attributed to the third person of the Trinity. It is the Holy Spirit, in particular, who applies Christ's work of redemption to those individuals elected in eternity past by the Father for salvation.

The response to the call, which the call itself brings into effect, is that the individual so called 'is thereby enabled to ... embrace the grace offered and conveyed in' the call. This embracing is another word for true, saving faith. It involves no work by which salvation is earned, nor any merit on the part of the sinner. It is a simple resting on Christ, a trusting in him and his work of redemption, for salvation.

As the call comes in the proclamation of the gospel (in whatever way that occurs in the life of each individual to whom it comes), the sinner, made alive and renewed by the Holy Spirit as they hear the call, is thereby enabled to respond to the Word proclaimed with true faith, turning from their sin to Christ alone. The Confession at this point underlines the tremendous power necessary to bring about such a change in the sinner, by comparing it (as Paul does in his letter to the Ephesians, 1:19–20) to the power that raised Jesus Christ from the dead. It is that same resurrection power that gives life to the dead sinner as they receive the effectual call of God.

Those incapable of being outwardly called (paragraph 3)

We have seen that the Confession expects those to whom the effectual call comes to 'answer this call' by embracing the gospel message with faith. What, then, about those who are mentally or otherwise incapable of such a response to the call? Can the call ever be effectual to them? The Confession answers that it can.

Firstly, paragraph 3 addresses the position of those who die in infancy. This could be seen, perhaps, to be a difficult question for Baptists, who reject the paedobaptist confidence in the covenant membership of their infant children. It might be thought, then, that Baptists would be more wary than their paedobaptist friends about affirming the equivalent statement in the Westminster Confession of Faith, which states, 'Elect infants, dying in infancy, are regenerated, and saved by Christ, through the Spirit'. In fact, however, the 1689 Confession repeats these words precisely, though it drops the references in the Westminster Confession to Luke 18:15–16 and Acts 2:38–39, classic texts relied upon for the paedobaptist position. Baptists, too, believe that infants can be regenerated and so saved.

There is no attempt to pinpoint who these elect infants might be. No conditions or characteristics are provided, other than that they are 'elect'.[1] Scripture gives little, if any, guidance on this matter. Knowing that 'the Judge of the whole earth' will always 'do what is just' (Gen. 18:25) and that our God is good and merciful and a God of grace, believers can, however, surely have hope that some infants will indeed be saved – and if they are saved, then by definition they are elect. That is all that can safely be said on the matter. As for how they are saved, it is rightly stated that they must be regenerated and that the Spirit works 'when, and where, and how he pleaseth', citing John 3:8. In other words, the entire subject is mysterious and is in the hands of the sovereign Lord who does all things well.

There are others, besides infants, who are unable to receive the external call of the word preached because, for example, they

---

1   The reprint of the 1689 Confession with a preface by C. H. Spurgeon omitted the word 'elect' from the beginning of this paragraph, in line with his conviction that all who die in infancy are regenerated and saved: *Thirty-Two Articles of Christian Faith and Practice, Or, Baptist Confession of Faith* (London: Alabaster & Passmore, 1855). Some more recent reprints and modernisations have repeated this omission.

suffer from severe learning difficulties. What of them? Again, paragraph 3 provides comfort. What is true of elect infants who die in infancy is equally true of 'all elect persons, who are incapable of being outwardly called by the ministry of the word'. This is the key: the normal means, as we have seen, whereby the call is brought to a person is the word preached and applied by the power of the Holy Spirit. The Spirit, in his sovereignty, is not tied exclusively to such means, however; where they are unsuited to a particular individual, due to that individual's capacity in some respect, the Spirit may use other means to make the call effective to them. Note that such people are still the object of the effectual call. They are called by the Spirit through such means as he chooses, no less than others; the difference is that, for these people, the call is exclusively inward and is not accompanied, as it normally would be, by a response to the outward call.

Those not elected (paragraph 4)

Chapter 10 finally addresses the position of those who are not elect. In short, the effectual call never comes to them. Paragraph 4 affirms that those who are not elect may well hear the external call of the word preached. They may also experience some 'common operations of the Spirit'. It is not specified what these might be, but we see evidence for such reactions in the Scriptures. Simon the magician, in Samaria, was amazed at the miracles that Philip was able to do. He is described as having 'believed' and was even baptised. Yet his later behaviour made clear that his profession has not involved regeneration. (Acts 8:9–13, 18–24). Simon had had some experience of the work of the Spirit – perhaps a measure of conviction, together with some impressions of the greatness and power of God – but not true conversion. The effectual call had not come to him. The writer to the Hebrews makes clear that apparently spiritual experiences of various kinds may come to those who ultimately show themselves never to have been the Lord's (Heb. 6:4–5).

The final statement of the chapter concerns the important question of those who do not profess to be Christians at all, but are nevertheless outwardly moral in character and behaviour and faithful to whatever religion they do hold. Many have thought that such people may well be saved, even though they make no claim to be Christian. Such a view is particularly popular today, but there were those even in the seventeenth century who were tempted to espouse it.

The Confession rejects such a possibility outright. However exemplary such a person might be in life and religion, they cannot be saved if the effectual call of the word and the Spirit has not come to them. That is plain from all that the Confession has already taught on human sinfulness after the fall: without the sovereign, gracious work of God in calling us effectually to saving faith in Christ, we are simply sinners guilty in the hands of a holy God, liable only to his condemnation and judgement.

Conclusion

The doctrine of effectual calling underlines that salvation is all of God. If anyone is to receive eternal life, it is the Lord who must accomplish it in full. Nothing must be left to the fallen human being, for if it were, it would fail. So mired are we in sin that we have neither the inclination nor the ability to turn to Christ, unless Christ first works it in us. That is precisely what he does when he effectually calls his elect to himself, by the word preached together with the secret, inward working of the Holy Spirit. As a result, all the elect, in due time, are regenerated and come to Christ in a saving manner. And all the glory goes to our triune God!

> Long my imprisoned spirit lay
>> fast bound in sin and nature's night;
> Thine eye diffused a quickening ray,
>> I woke, the dungeon flamed with light;
> my chains fell off, my heart was free,
>> I rose, went forth, and followed Thee.

> Charles Wesley

Study questions

1. Think carefully about the various things that God does in the elect when he calls them effectively, as stated in paragraph 1. How do these relate to your own experience?

2. If we are 'wholly passive' in the work of the effectual call, as paragraph 2 says, why does Scripture call upon the unbeliever to repent and believe in Christ (see also chapter 20, paragraph 4)?

3. How might we seek to comfort a believer whose infant has died?

Further reading

Jeremy Walker, *Anchored in Grace: Fixed Points for Humble Faith* (Cruciform, 2015)

Paul Helm, *The Callings: The Gospel in the World* (Edinburgh: Banner of Truth, 1987), pp. 1-12

A. W. Pink, *The Sovereignty of God* (rev. edn., Edinburgh, Banner of Truth, 1961), pp. 67-80

Chapters 11 – 13:
Justification, Adoption & Sanctification

What does it really mean to be a Christian? How does God view the believer? And how is the Christian life to be lived? Can the believer totally conquer sin in his life? If and when we do fall into sin, what is the effect on our relationship with God? These and other vital questions about the life of faith are addressed by the teaching of Scripture on justification, adoption and sanctification. These are the subjects of chapters 11, 12 and 13, respectively, of the 1689 Confession.

These chapters are much needed today. There is a great deal of confusion on these topics, even among evangelicals, caused by a lack of clear teaching in the church. As a result, many believers are unsure about their salvation and their spiritual growth is stunted. The church urgently needs to recover a clear understanding of the biblical teaching in these vital areas. These chapters of the 1689 Confession are an excellent tool to help achieve this.

Justification (chapter 11)

What is justification?

The first way in which these chapters help is simply by devoting separate chapters to justification and sanctification respectively. One of the most common and harmful mistakes that Christians make is to confuse these two essential aspects of Christ's work of salvation. We do this whenever we think that the work of justification involves any kind of change in us or any level of contributory work from us. The first paragraph of chapter 11 rejects any such idea by a series of clear, negative statements.

Firstly, it tells us that God justifies the believer 'not by infusing righteousness into them'. It is a common error to believe that justification involves moral change in the Christian and that God forgives sin, at least in part, on the basis of that moral change. This is to confuse justification and sanctification – something that the Roman Catholic Church does in its doctrine of justification – and is a serious and fundamental error in the understanding of the biblical teaching on the subject. Justification involves no moral change of any kind in the person justified.

Secondly, justification does not result from or depend upon anything that we do. As paragraph 1 of chapter 11 puts it, justification is 'not for any thing wrought in [the one justified], or done by them'. This addresses another very common mistake on this topic, that we can – or must – in some way contribute something, however small, towards our justification.

No, says the Confession, in line with Scripture, we contribute nothing at all. This is a great relief, because anything that we might contribute would undoubtedly be spoiled by sin and defective; it would therefore be ineffective and our justification would fail. Yet Christians are constantly plagued by the thought that they might not have done enough to be truly acceptable before God. As a result, their prayer life and their service to the Lord are not what they could be, to their great loss.

A final error that paragraph 1 refutes is the popular idea that God counts our faith, or any act of obedience, as righteousness. Some want to turn faith into a work: faith becomes the contribution that we make towards our salvation. Others have argued that our own good works, the fruit of saving faith, are counted by God as righteousness to us. In rejecting these, paragraph 1 states that the believer is justified 'not by imputing faith itself, the act of believing, or any other evangelical obedience to them, as their righteousness'. Justification does not come to us on the basis of anything at all that we do or contribute, not even our faith.

Justification is, rather, based on something done entirely outside of us, by someone completely different. It is, as Martin Luther put it, an 'alien righteousness', that is, the righteousness of another. That other is, of course, the Lord Jesus Christ. Our justification depends totally on the perfect life and death of Christ, who 'by his obedience and death did fully discharge the debt of all those that are justified'. Christ's death on the cross – his sacrifice of himself and shedding of his blood – fully and perfectly satisfied the justice of God for us who believe.

That death was thus both penal and substitutionary – 'undergoing in their stead the penalty due unto them'. Christ's death was not simply an exhibition of supreme love; nor did it merely provide sinners with the opportunity to be saved, if they would only believe. Christ's death actually accomplished something, in and of itself – it satisfied the justice of God that would otherwise have demanded from his sinful people the full measure due for their sins. His death paid for our sins in full.

As a result, salvation is, as paragraph 3 states, 'only of free grace, that both the exact justice and rich grace of God might be glorified in the justification of sinners'. It is this great work of Christ – his obedience in his life and his death – that has won us justification, not anything at all that we have done. This is very good news indeed, for there is no defect or failing of any kind in what Christ has accomplished. It is therefore the perfect basis for justification and, if it is accounted to us, we cannot fail to be justified, perfectly and for ever.

Justification is, according to paragraph 1, 'for Christ's sake alone' and God justifies 'by imputing Christ's active obedience unto the whole law, and passive obedience in his death, for their whole and sole righteousness'. Some Christians have questioned whether Christ's obedience is indeed imputed to the believer. They argue that surely the forgiveness of sins is sufficient. The old catchphrase reflects this idea: justification means that God views me 'just-as-if I'd never sinned'.

Justification does indeed involve the forgiveness of sins, as paragraph 1 affirms, but that on its own would be insufficient to give us a title to eternal life and the glories of heaven. For that, we need a positive righteousness – and one that is as perfect as the obedience of Jesus Christ who perfectly did the will of His Father and obeyed the whole law. And that is precisely what we are given in Christ, when we are justified.

And so, states paragraph 1, God justifies 'by pardoning their sins and by accounting and accepting their persons as righteous'. That is what justification means to the believer who stands before God forgiven of all sins and treated as perfectly righteous in His sight.

Who is justified?

The Bible is not universalist and never holds out the hope that everyone will be saved. Who then is justified? Chapter 11 answers this vital question in a number of different ways.

Firstly, we must believe – justification is by faith. Yet the relationship between justification and faith needs careful definition. Simply to state that we are 'justified by faith', while true, is inadequate as a comprehensive statement of the relevant truth. The Confession is therefore very careful in its pronouncements about faith as it relates to justification. Three important points emerge from chapter 11.

1. Faith involves 'receiving and resting' on Christ and his righteousness. It is passive, not active. It is not a work, as we have seen, and does not contribute in any meritorious sense to justification. It takes our dependence for justification completely off ourselves and places it entirely upon Christ. It denies any place for any righteousness of our own, of any kind, in justification and admits Christ's righteousness as our 'whole and sole righteousness'.

2. Faith is a gift of God. We do not produce it from within ourselves, nor can we. We do not have the resources to contribute anything even to this faith – it must come to us entirely from God.

3. Faith is always accompanied by 'all other saving graces' – it is never alone, though it is 'the alone instrument of

justification'. This faith is 'no dead faith, but worketh by love'. It is vital to affirm this, on two different fronts:

i. On the one hand, the instrument of justification – the means by which it is communicated to us by Christ – is faith and faith alone. That faith is a simple trust – a resting or receiving, as we have already seen. It does not include love or hope or any other grace; nor does it include any work. It is, for that purpose, alone.

ii. On the other hand, that faith is never alone, because all other graces and good works always accompany it. This is James's argument, in the second chapter of his New Testament letter. Faith that does not produce good works is a dead faith, of no value for justification or for anything else. Saving faith, by contrast, will be accompanied by love, hope and other graces, resulting in good works. This is the biblical teaching that the Confession seeks to uphold and to which we must adhere.

It is those who believe, then, who are justified. But the Confession also describes the justified in terms of their election. In fact, God's sovereign choice of his people is the prime category by which chapter 11 distinguishes those who are justified from those who are not. It begins with this resounding affirmation: 'Those whom God effectually calleth, he also freely justifieth'. As well as providing an obvious link to chapter 10, on effectual calling, this plainly establishes that it is the elect, and only the elect, who receive the blessing of justification. So paragraph 4 states, 'God did from all eternity decree to justify all the elect'.

As justification is truly a free gift, entirely of grace and not dependent in any way on us, it could only be by God's eternal decree that some could be justified and not others. This has led some to conclude, wrongly, that the elect are justified from eternity past and that all that happens when they are converted is that they come to realise that they are already justified. Others have held, in a similar fashion, that justification occurred for all the elect when Christ died.

It is true that justification is rooted in God's eternal election and that Christ's work on the basis of which the elect are justified was completed at the cross. Nevertheless, the Scriptures consistently refer to the believer's justification as being 'by faith' – faith is the instrument by which justification is actually applied to and received by the individual; before that time, we were, as Paul told the Ephesians, 'dead in your trespasses and sins' and 'by nature children under wrath as the others were also' (Eph. 2:1, 3).

Chapter 11 therefore affirms that the elect 'are not justified personally, until the Holy Spirit doth in due time actually apply Christ unto them' (paragraph 4) – in other words, until they come, by the regenerating power of the Spirit, to saving faith and repentance. It is then, and not before, that they are justified.

What happens, though, when someone who is justified by faith falls into sin? Some fear that they could fall from grace, depending on the seriousness of their sin or the length of time for which the sin continues. Others can be very arrogant, believing that sin cannot affect their spiritual state in any way, because Christ is their righteousness. The result can be a severe lack of assurance or an offensive presumption. Either way, spiritual life suffers.

Chapter 11 provides the biblical response to this question, which is that the believer's justified status is in no way impaired by his sins, but his communion with God may well be (paragraph 5). It is true that, because our justification rests on Christ alone, it can never be diminished, spoiled or lost. But our sense of fellowship with God can certainly suffer all those things, because of our sins. Sin may bring us under God's 'fatherly displeasure'; we lose the sense of his comforting presence; prayer becomes very hard, as do other spiritual activities. Those in this condition must 'humble themselves, confess their sins, beg pardon, and renew their faith and repentance', in order that 'the light of [God's] countenance' may be restored to them.

Finally, the Confession clarifies that all the principles concerning justification apply equally to Old as to New Testament believers (paragraph 6).

Adoption (chapter 12)

Following the chapter on justification is one on adoption, made up of just one paragraph. Adoption is a neglected topic among Christians, to our great loss. It is a vital and most encouraging aspect of the fruit of Christ's work of redemption for his people.

The chapter on adoption follows immediately after the chapter on justification, so as to affirm that adoption is a blessing true of every believer. It is not only for the spiritually advanced, or for those who have reached a certain level of spiritual understanding or maturity. 'All those that are justified', begins the chapter, partake, by the grace of God, in adoption. This means that we become a child of God and enjoy all the 'liberties and privileges' which flow from that status. These are summarised in the chapter as follows.

1. God places his name upon us. This indicates that we belong to him and that he is pleased to own his fatherly relationship to us. It implies a promise of his care and protection and suggests that his character will be reflected in us, as we are conformed to Christ through the ministry of word and Spirit.

2. He gives us the Spirit of adoption, which is the Holy Spirit who dwells within each believer. By him, we 'are enabled to cry Abba Father' – in prayer, to address almighty God as our heavenly father, with the same intimacy of relationship that a child is able to address his human father. This is not an infantile term such as 'daddy', but the word that a mature Jewish adult would use to speak to his father, just as Jesus did in addressing his heavenly Father.

3. We thereby have 'access to the throne of grace'. This underlines the privilege of prayer for the believer: that we have direct access, through Christ and by the Spirit, to the Father who sits on the throne of heaven itself, governing all things. We do not have to go through any other individual – not a priest, nor the pastor, nor anyone else. We do not have to wait until a church service or some special religious occasion. We are not obliged to go through particular ceremonies or rites, in order to approach God's throne. We may come at any time and place, in any circumstances, to speak to God, because he is our Father and we are his children. This is an extraordinary and most glorious privilege.

4. God our Father pities us – he has compassion upon us in all our troubles and sufferings. We can turn to him and find help in all such circumstances, without fail. He also protects us – from enemies who want to harm us and from all evil that would destroy us. This does not mean that we live trouble-free lives, for the Bible makes clear that believers will suffer in this life. It means that nothing that comes against us can ultimately take from us the blessings that God has for us and that all that happens to us is under his sovereign control and, ultimately, for our good. And he provides for us, so that we do not need to fear or become anxious about our needs in this life. He also chastens us, as any good father does, for our disobedience; this is not pleasant, but it is, again, for our good and for his glory.

5. In all this, the child of God can be confident that his heavenly Father will never cast him off. Rather, he can be sure that he is sealed – assuredly God's, kept by him – until Christ returns, 'the day of redemption', when he will 'inherit the promises, as heirs, of everlasting salvation'. If the ruler of the heavens and the earth is indeed our Father, what else would we expect?

Sanctification (chapter 13)

For Christians, there is great blessing to be found in the wonderfully rich biblical truths of our justification and divine adoption, and it is equally so when when it comes to our sanctification. There are, however, a variety of unbiblical ideas about sanctification which the Confession helps us to address.

There are those who teach that sinlessness (at some level) is an achievable goal, at least theoretically, for the believer in this life: the Wesley brothers and, more recently, Watchman Nee gave teaching of this kind. Some hold that, through one or more special experiences from God, a believer may be raised to a higher level of spirituality which gives greater, or possibly even complete, victory over sin.

At the other extreme, there are those who believe that our sins are of little or no consequence, because the righteousness of Christ is imputed to us. God therefore, they say, does not see our sin, nor does he in any way consider us as sinners or as sinful, but only as entirely righteous before him.

One or other of these errors will lead the believer either to great distress and despair or to great complacency and presumption. For many Christians, who do not believe either of these extremes, the daily struggle with sin nevertheless tends to induce in them feelings of hopelessness and failure, because of their frequent defeats. This robs them of spiritual assurance and joy in Christ.

All this is the result of poor or erroneous teaching on the subject of sanctification. Our Puritan and Baptist forebears, in their framing of the various reformed confessions of the seventeenth century, had a far better and more biblical approach. Christians who grasp the scriptural truths set out in chapter 13 of the 1689 Confession will have a proper foundation on which to build their lives as believers in this fallen world. They will learn how the battle with sin is to be conducted and what they should expect in terms of victory or otherwise in that battle.

The chapter is made up of three paragraphs, which set out the three vital truths that need to be understood.

1. The chapter begins by describing the believer as one who is 'united to Christ', as well as 'effectually called', regenerate and so with a new heart and spirit, on the basis of Christ's death and resurrection. This is the foundation of the work of sanctification, which would otherwise be impossible. The believer is not sanctified by any resources originally in himself, but on the basis of all that God has done for him in Christ and by the Holy Spirit.

   So those who are born again of the Spirit of God experience some genuine success in the battle with sin. They are 'farther sanctified' – implying the truth that their regeneration and union with Christ in themselves constitute an initial sanctification that is 'really and personally' – so, in contrast with justification, sanctification brings about a true inward change.

   There are three aspects to this work: the destruction of the dominion of sin – that is, a definitive break with the overriding mastery that sin enjoyed over the believer before conversion; the weakening and mortifying of the lusts; and the enlivening and strengthening of the saving graces. The goal is 'the practice of all true holiness, without which no man shall see the Lord'.

   Crucially, the paragraph informs us that this work progresses 'by [Christ's] word and Spirit' indwelling the believer – thus the ministry of the word of God in the power of the Spirit is essential for the work of sanctification. It is a question of our mind, heart and will being increasingly formed according to the pattern of Christ, by means of the

Spirit-anointed teaching of the Scriptures, in the regular ministry of the local church.

2. The second paragraph makes clear, however, that the work of sanctification is 'imperfect in this life'. This is because of 'some remnants of corruption' that survive in every part of the believer. As a result, there is 'a continual and irreconcilable war; the flesh lusting against the Spirit, and the Spirit against the flesh'. This is the reality of the believer's experience throughout his life on this earth. The hope of being lifted above this battle onto a higher plane of spiritual existence is totally vain – it will never happen in this life. We must steel ourselves for the continual, daily struggle with sin.

3. The chapter ends on a positive note, assuring the believer that the Spirit of Christ continually supplies strength for the battle. Even so, the corruption remaining in the Christian 'for a time may much prevail': quick victories are not guaranteed and there may be many slips and falls along the way. Nevertheless, the believer is to expect some progress over the long term. The Christian should 'grow in grace, perfecting holiness in the fear of God, pressing after an heavenly life, in evangelical obedience to all the commands' of Christ in his word.

The progress in sanctification of which chapter 13 speaks can be hard to see in reality, because it occurs over the long term and is so frequently punctuated by defeats, both small and, sometimes, great. Our daily experience, as the second paragraph suggests, tends to be that of struggle and, often, defeat. It is not by any means one of constant victory. The chapter recognises this, as does Scripture, and we should take courage from this, without becoming complacent.

The battle with sin will continue until the moment of death itself, but we are not to lose heart, remembering the completeness of our justification and the continued supply of the strength of God's Spirit for the fight.

Conclusion

These three chapters of the 1689 Confession form the core of the application of Christ's work of redemption to his elect people in this life. The essence of that work consists in the three topics covered here: justification, adoption and sanctification. Believers who study the teaching of these chapters carefully, in the light of God's word, will grow in their assurance of salvation and in their understanding of the ongoing battle with sin. They will have a firmer grasp of their status as a child of God and of the enormous privileges that that brings. Although grieving over their sin and experiencing continued repentance for it, they will experience greater peace in their experience of communion with their triune God and will be able to rejoice with deeper and greater joy at all that Christ has done for them.

God's children rest in the finished nature of the work of salvation and seek by word and Spirit to grow in grace, they will serve Christ and others faithfully and be able to look forward, by the grace of God alone, to the inheritance that is laid up in heaven for them.

My hope is built on nothing less
than Jesus' blood and righteousness;
I dare not trust the sweetest frame,
but wholly lean on Jesus' name.
> On Christ, the solid rock, I stand;
> all other ground is sinking sand.

Edward Mote

Study questions

1. How real is the doctrine of justification by faith to you? Do you consider yourself constantly to be, by faith in Christ, justified before the Father? How can you grow in your grasp of this truth?

2. When the devil accuses us with thoughts of our own inadequacy and tempts us to give up or doubt our salvation, how can this doctrine help us?

3. How much do you think about the truth of adoption? What difference would it make to your life as a believer if you pondered it more?

Further reading

Maurice Roberts, *Finding Peace with God* (Banner of Truth, 2013)

John Murray, *Redemption Accomplished and Applied* (Banner of Truth, 1979)

John Owen, 'The Doctrine of Justification by Faith', *Works*, vol. 5 (repr. Banner of Truth, 1965)

Sinclair Ferguson, *John Owen on the Christian Life* (Banner of Truth, 1987)

Chapters 14 – 16:
Faith, Repentance & Good Works

Chapter 8 of the Confession – a pivotal chapter – expounded the work that Christ accomplished as mediator, once and for all, for the salvation of the elect. In chapters 10 to 13, the Confession addressed the ongoing work of Christ by his Spirit to apply that work to his elect, in effectual calling, justification, adoption and sanctification. Now the Confession tells us how God brings about in the elect a saving response to Christ's work, in faith, repentance and good works.

Saving faith (chapter 14)

Evangelicals know that it is faith alone in Christ alone that saves, without works or merit on our part; that faith is a gift from God that is worked in our hearts by his Spirit and not something that we obtain from our own resources; and that faith is not itself a work, but simply the receiving of the grace that God grants to sinners in and through Jesus Christ. Chapter 14 of the Confession affirms all these truths. But this chapter teaches other important truths about saving faith.

Beginning and growth of faith (paragraph 1)

Chapter 14 opens with the plain statement that saving faith 'is the work of the Spirit of Christ in their hearts'. It does not come from us, but from the Lord. We do not have the resources in ourselves to produce faith. No act of our will, no unaided desire of our own, no expression of emotion can produce saving faith in us. It is the gift of God – the 'grace of faith' is the Confession's phrase here – which he bestows upon the elect in his good time.

This normally comes through the ministry of the word of God – that is, as we hear the Bible preached, taught, opened up, explained and applied in the regular worship of the church. This may happen in other contexts – in a small group, or in a personal conversation, or through hearing something on the radio or internet – but the normal means is through the preached word in the ordinary meetings of the gathered church.

This faith can (and should) grow. Paul writes to the Corinthians about the increase of their faith (2 Cor. 10:15). Faith can be small and weak or it can grow and be strong. How does this happen? The Confession makes clear that, again, we cannot do this ourselves, but rather that it is done to us: saving faith 'is increased and strengthened' in the believer. The one who causes this to happen is the Spirit of Christ. This does not mean that we are to be inactive. God in his goodness has provided the means whereby our faith is to grow and we are to make use of those means.

Those means are, firstly, again, the ministry of the word, as this first paragraph states. It goes on to list other means that God has appointed for the increase of our faith: baptism, the Lord's Supper and prayer. The list is not exhaustive. We are not to neglect any means that God has appointed for our good.

This has very practical consequences. It means that Christians are to place themselves (and their families) under sound biblical ministry in the context of membership of a faithful local church, submitting themselves to the care, oversight and discipline of that church. It means listening carefully to the preachers and teachers of the church as they minister the word, week by week, and seek to lead the church according to that word. It means believing the word, as it is so preached and applied, seeking to put it into practice day by day. It means being baptised and participating regularly in the church's observation of the Lord's Supper. It means an active, faithful prayer life. This is how our faith grows.

How does faith relate to the Scriptures and to Christ? (paragraph 2)

Christians sometimes ask, what is the minimum amount of truth needed in order to be saved? Does one need to believe that Jesus is fully divine? Is a correct understanding of the doctrine of justification by faith alone required? What if someone is unclear on the inerrancy of Scripture?

This chapter of the Confession does not quite answer these questions, but it does tell us what saving faith should result in: by such faith, it says, a Christian comes to believe all the Scriptures to be true, on the basis that the Scriptures speak with the authority of God himself. Saving faith also produces in the believer a sense of the excellency of the Bible, above all other books and everything else in the whole world. By faith, we see the Scriptures teaching us about God – his glory and attributes; about Christ – his nature and offices; and about the Holy Spirit – his power and fullness. The working out of our faith is wonderfully trinitarian.

This in turn has practical results. As by faith believers see these truths more and more in Scripture, they find that they can cast their 'Soul upon the truth thus believed' – they really do trust what it teaches and can found their life upon it. They also find that they respond differently – and appropriately – to different kinds of teaching in Scripture. To commands, they give obedience; where the Bible threatens, they tremble; when it gives promises, they embrace them, both for this life and for eternity. But the main effect relates to Christ himself, as the next section will explain.

Is faith more than intellectual assent? (paragraph 2)

Christmas Evans was a great preacher and evangelist in Wales in the late eighteenth and early nineteenth centuries. He was full of life and love for Christ. Yet for a few years, from 1796 to 1802, he found his heart cold, his soul dry and his Christian life robbed of joy. His prayers lacked power and he ceased to experience God's presence. Evans traced the problem back to the error taught by some Baptists in north Wales, where he lived, who believed that saving faith consisted simply in intellectual assent to the foundational truths of the gospel. So long as you affirmed that what the Bible taught about Christ and salvation was true, you were a Christian, according to these 'Scotch Baptists' or 'Sandemanians' (after Robert Sandeman, who popularised this idea, and those Baptists in Scotland who espoused it).

One day, Evans was climbing the mountain of Cader Idris in north Wales, on his way south to preach. He caught sight of the snow and ice towards the summit and was overcome by the sense of his own recent coldness of heart. He began to cry out to the Lord, who came afresh to him with an overwhelming experience of his love and presence. The preacher renounced the error that he had espoused. Saving faith involves more than mere intellectual assent.

The foundational gospel truths must certainly be known and understood in order for there to be true faith. Those truths must also receive the clear and firm assent of the mind. But there is a third, essential element to saving faith. The Confession teaches that saving faith involves 'accepting, receiving, and resting upon [Christ] alone, for justification, sanctification, and eternal life, by virtue of the covenant of grace'. This is expressed in Scripture in terms of coming to Christ, feeding on Christ, believing on him (Mt. 11:28; Jn. 6:35, 50; 14:11). The idea behind these different terms is the same: there must be a whole-hearted casting of oneself upon Christ for salvation. The believer rests confidently and permanently upon Christ and his work of salvation. This is the essence of faith.

There is another, related error into which some fall, which is at the opposite extreme from that which ensnared Christmas Evans. That is to put one's trust in feelings or experience, rather than directly on Christ, to see whether one is saved. Some calvinistic Baptists have been particularly prone to this error. They want to see various defined marks in themselves – of a sufficiently deep work of conviction, or some inward sense of the Lord's favour or blessing in their soul – before they will believe that they are really the Lord's. While there is a place for self-examination, the tendency of Scripture is to point us to Christ for assurance of our salvation. Within us, we see only rottenness and corruption, which is of no help to us. In Christ, by contrast, we see all that we need to be saved for eternity. We look to him, then, affirming the truths of the gospel and trusting entirely in him for our salvation and all that that involves. That is saving faith.

How strong does faith need to be? (paragraph 3)

Some Christians worry that they do not have 'enough faith' to be saved; or they think that the stronger their faith, the more likely they are to be saved. But Jesus taught that even the smallest degree of faith – even if it is as small as a grain of mustard seed – is sufficient to move a mountain (Mt. 17:20). Of course, Jesus was not interested in his disciples literally moving mountains. He was teaching them that what ultimately matters, when it comes to faith, is its quality rather than its quantity.

If you have genuine, saving faith, even in the smallest quantity, you are saved. This is because it is not, strictly speaking, your faith that saves you, but Christ. It is his work of redemption that saves; our faith is simply the instrument by which we, by his grace, take possession of the salvation that he has won – the hand that receives the gift. And so long as that hand has truly taken what is offered freely to it, it matters not how weak or small the hand may be.

This is why the Confession draws a clear boundary between saving faith, whether weak or strong, and what it calls the faith of 'temporary believers' (paragraph 3). There is a kind of believing that does not save and does not last. It comes from within us, not from heaven. Jesus referred to this in the parable of the sower, when he spoke of the seed falling on stony ground – those who receive the word with joy, but do not last when troubles come. This is not a weak version of saving faith; it is not saving faith at all. It is of an entirely different nature from such faith; it is not the work of the Holy Spirit and it is only temporary.

In contrast, true faith perseveres. Saving faith may often be subjected to trials and may at times actually weaken, but it always 'gets the victory', as the Confession puts it – it wins through. This is one of the great characteristics of true faith: it does not ultimately fail. That is why the believer must make use of the means of grace so that faith may grow. Many believers thereby attain a 'full assurance' – a state in which they are sure, by the Spirit, that they are indeed saved and a child of God. The subject of assurance is addressed more fully in chapter 18. This chapter 14, on saving faith, concludes by reminding us that all this occurs 'through Christ, who is both the author and the finisher of our faith'.

Repentance to life and salvation (chapter 15)

The Savoy Declaration, which this chapter of the 1689 Confession follows almost word for word, rewrote the equivalent chapter of the Westminster Confession practically in its entirety. The reasons for this are obscure, but seem likely to be connected with a contemporary debate that the leading congregationalist theologian of the day, John Owen, was engaged in. This was about the status of infants in relation to salvation. Owen, who is probably behind the wording of the Savoy document, was eager to articulate the truth that elect infants dying in infancy are the subject of regeneration, but do not need to repent as they are not guilty of personal sin. Hence the first paragraph of this chapter, like that in the Savoy

Declaration, relates repentance to those 'converted at riper years', probably meaning those of an age at which repentance becomes possible and necessary for salvation.[1]

Repentance is the neglected twin brother of saving faith. A study of the way in which the preachers of the New Testament exhorted their hearers in their evangelistic messages soon shows that sometimes they urged faith (Paul in the Philippian jail, Acts 16:31) and sometimes repentance (Peter in Jerusalem on the Day of Pentecost, Acts 2:38). They are two sides of the same coin. It is not possible to have one without the other. Saving faith is a repentant faith and true repentance looks believingly to Christ.

It is, however, easier to talk and preach about faith than it is about repentance. Faith is warm and positive; it means coming to Christ and this is pleasant to commend. Repentance, by contrast, is essentially negative and more difficult to preach, as it relates directly to our sin and calls for deep humility on our part. For these reasons, repentance can easily be wrongly neglected in our evangelism and our preaching.

A lack of emphasis on repentance has two very serious effects. Firstly, it severely weakens our evangelism. The call to faith is a call to repent – to turn from sin. Without the latter, the former can easily degrade into a form of decisionism, in which individuals believe that they have become Christians simply by some act – maybe a prayer, or by raising a hand in a meeting – indicating a desire to identify with Christ. If our evangelism includes no instruction on the need for repentance, the danger is that our hearers will not

---

1 I am grateful to Dr James Renihan for his insights on this issue – see his *Confessing the Faith. Vol. 2. The Second London Baptist Confession of Faith* (Macclesfield: Broken Wharfe, 2022), pp. 368-74.

realise that any serious change in their lifestyle is required. It is quite likely, then, that any supposed profession of faith will in fact not be true conversion to Christ at all, but will simply produce a religious hypocrite who is likely at some point to fall away from his profession.

The second effect of a failure adequately to teach repentance concerns believers. As the chapter points out, believers continue to sin throughout their lives and even the 'best of men' may 'fall into great sins and provocations' (paragraph 2). What does the believer do when this happens? If he or she has no sound grasp of the doctrine of repentance, the result is likely to be either despair or backsliding. The believer who is ignorant of the provision that Christ has 'mercifully provided' in the covenant of grace will not be sure what to do when they fall into sin. Not knowing that Christ has provided for them to 'be renewed through repentance unto salvation' (paragraph 2), they may be driven to question whether they are truly saved at all. And in the seeming absence of an effective remedy for their sin, they may fall further and further into it until they are in a truly backslidden state.

Any neglect of biblical teaching on repentance in our churches is thus a severe reproach to us and needs to be remedied speedily. This may be done, as recommended by this chapter, through the 'constant preaching of repentance' (paragraph 5), which perfectly addresses the need which all believers have due to their sin – for all sins, even the smallest, deserve damnation, but there is 'no sin so great, that it shall bring damnation on them that repent' (paragraph 5). It is therefore the duty of believers to repent 'through the whole course of our lives' (paragraph 4).

This raises the question, what is true repentance? The chapter defines it as an 'evangelical grace' (paragraph 3), which distinguishes it from what is sometimes called 'legal' repentance. The latter is what Paul refers to when he wrote to the Corinthians of a repentance leading only to 'worldly grief' which 'produces death' (2 Cor. 7:10). It is a repentance that is induced merely by a fear of punishment or of other unwanted consequences of sin. Unlike evangelical repentance, it does not look to Christ and is not joined with saving faith. True repentance, by contrast, 'leads to salvation without regret', as the apostle says. Such repentance comes to the unbeliever at his conversion as part of God's effectual calling of him by the Spirit (paragraph 1). Like faith, repentance is not a work that contributes to our salvation in any meritorious way; it is a gift of God.

The Confession in paragraph 3 of this chapter details the following elements of the evangelical grace of repentance:

- it is a work of the Holy Spirit;
- it brings a sense of the 'manifold evils of his sin';
- it operates by faith in Christ;
- it leads to humility, godly sorrow, hatred of the sin and abhorrence of self;
- it is accompanied by prayer for pardon and 'strength of grace';
- it is marked by a desire induced by the Spirit to walk before God in his ways in everything.

The following paragraph adds to these elements by making clear the need to repent of 'particular known sins, particularly' – general expressions of regret for sin are insufficient. The believer will in fact tend to think that their repentance is never sufficient and in this they are quite correct. Because our salvation is not earned by repentance, this does not, however, jeopardise our eternal state, for that is dependent upon Christ alone. As with faith, the vital question is the quality, rather than the quantity, of our repentance: is it evangelical, reflecting the above elements, rather than legal?

The Confession's description demonstrates the richness of true repentance. Biblical repentance, though exacting, provides just the remedy that the believer needs for his ongoing sin, whether small or great. In the same way that serious illness may require a course of strong medicine, or maybe even invasive medical treatment, our sin cannot be lightly cured. Sin in the believer is offensive and displeasing to a holy God. Although its guilt and power are fully dealt with by Christ's death on the cross, the damaging effects of sin on the conscience, on our habits and manner of life, on our communion with God and our service to him day by day mean that nothing less than the kind of repentance described here will be sufficient to renew and restore us and enable us to continue to grow in Christ.

Good works (chapter 16)

Again, evangelicals know well that our good works contribute nothing to our salvation, that the outworking of saving faith involves good works and that it is God himself who by his Spirit gives us the power to perform good works of any kind. This chapter teaches each of those truths clearly (paragraphs 5, 2 and 3, respectively). A number of significant questions, however, remain.

What are good works? (paragraph 1)

Few, perhaps, stop to ask this question. We assume that we know the answer, but do we? Good works are those defined as such by Scripture: they are 'only such as God hath commanded in his holy word'. This makes sense, as it is God who defines what is good and he alone is good (Lk. 18:19). He commands that we be good and tells us in the Bible what we are to do to that end. Our good intentions alone do not make an act good. Nor should we imagine that a deed is good because we have a tremendous inward sense that we should do it (which the Confession calls 'blind zeal').

What benefits do good works bring? (paragraph 2)

Good works obviously help those for whom they are done. Beyond that, the chapter tells us that they are the 'fruits and evidences of a true and lively faith'. This is valuable as a help towards assurance that one is truly the Lord's. In addition, such works show that we are thankful to the Lord, they build up other believers, they make Christian witness attractive, they silence critics and bring glory to God who is the workman behind the works. Good works constitute the necessary fruit which issues in (though does not earn) eternal life.

Diligence in good works (paragraph 3)

If our good works are the result of the operations of the Spirit of God in and through us, so that our ability to do those works is 'wholly from the Spirit of Christ', can we simply sit back and, as it were, let them happen? No, says the Confession: this truth does not allow us to 'grow negligent'. Though the grace and strength to perform good works comes from the Holy Spirit, we are the ones who are actually to do those works. And we are not to wait for some specific inward prompting of the Spirit before we engage in good works. Rather, we are to be diligent in 'stirring up the grace of God' within us, so that we might further pursue good works.

How does God view our good works? (paragraphs 4 to 6)

We can never fulfil our duties of obedience to God; we always fall short of what is required of us (paragraph 4). We know that our works contribute nothing by way of merit to our salvation and that all such works of ours are defiled by and mixed with weakness and imperfection (paragraph 5). How then does God view our good works? Are they in any sense acceptable to him?

The Confession affirms that, in so far as they are the work of believers, God does accept them. The reason is connected with the believer's union with Christ. Because God accepts the believer in Christ, he also accepts his works in Christ. This is not because they are without defect or beyond reproach, for they are not, but because God looks upon them 'in his Son' and so 'is pleased to accept and reward that which is sincere', though imperfect (paragraph 6). This is most reassuring. It strengthens faith and provides a great spur to good works.

What about the good works of unbelievers? (paragraph 7)

Do the good works of unbelievers have any value? The answer of the Confession is that they may indeed do good to others and this may also be useful to the doers, but because they lack faith and are not done in accordance with God's word and for his glory, they do not please him and are sinful. Even so, it is still more sinful for such works to be neglected.

Conclusion

These chapters of the Confession outline the essential truths concerning the response of the elect to the saving work of Christ, as they experience the effectual call of the Spirit in their lives regenerating them and bringing them to the Saviour. The result of that work is that they repent and believe in Christ in a saving manner and their lives thereafter show the fruit of that work in their good works. This is all due to the work of God alone, in Christ and by the Holy Spirit, and so all the glory is also due to him alone.

> With broken heart and contrite sigh,
> a trembling sinner, Lord, I cry;
> Your pardoning grace is rich and free,
> O God, be merciful to me!

> Cornelius Elven

Study questions

1. Think about Christmas Evans's experience of Sandemanianism and ask yourself whether you have ever been through a similar period of dry intellectualism. How can you better nurture the growth of your faith in Christ?

2. Ask yourself in the light of chapter 15 how seriously you take evangelical repentance and how you would deepen your experience of true repentance.

3. There are countless good works that we might do in our life. How do we know which we should do? In what areas of your life are good works lacking?

Further reading

C. H. Spurgeon, *Faith: What It Is and What It Leads To* (repr. Christian Focus, 2011)

Thomas Watson, *The Doctrine of Repentance* (repr. Banner of Truth, 1987)

Jeremy Walker, *What is Repentance?* (Reformation Heritage, 2015)

Mark Jones, *A Christian's Pocket Guide to Good Works and Rewards: In This Life and the Next* (Christian Focus, 2017)

John Owen, *The Mortification of Sin* (abridged, Banner of Truth, 2004)

Chapters 17 & 18:
Perseverance & Assurance

Perseverance and assurance are doctrines of great comfort and joy to the believer in Christ. They have also been the subject of much controversy and difficulty. Roman Catholic theology opposes them; Arminianism questions or denies them. Both those systems thereby rob believers of the joy and certain hope of eternal salvation that the Bible promises. No doubt this is one reason why these truths are so clearly stated in the 1689 Confession, as they are in the Westminster Confession of Faith and the Savoy Declaration of Faith and Order.

The perseverance of the saints (chapter 17)

The doctrine of the perseverance of the saints, as expressed in paragraph 1 of chapter 17 of the Confession, states that the genuine believer in Christ 'shall certainly persevere [in the state of grace] to the end and be eternally saved'. They will without doubt win their eternal inheritance. Nothing can prevent that, for they are 'accepted in the beloved', that is, Christ, 'called and sanctified by his Spirit, and given the precious faith of his elect', grand truths that have been addressed in previous chapters. The Confession cites Jesus' words in John 10:28–29 to support this teaching, where Jesus says, 'I give them ['my sheep', v. 27] eternal life, and they will never perish. No one will snatch them out of my hand. My Father, who has given them to me, is greater than all. No one is able to snatch them out of the Father's hand.'

The promise of final perseverance is underlined in those verses by Jesus' double affirmation of the absolute security of his sheep, coupled with his assertion that in this vital matter (as in all others) he and the Father are completely united (as he goes on to say in the verse that follows, 'I and the Father are one'). Paul's statement to the Philippian church is also cited: 'I am sure of this, that he who started a good work in you will carry it on to completion until the day of Christ Jesus' (Phil. 1:6). Other verses, such as John 6:37, 39 and Jesus' prayer in John 17:24, could be mentioned in support. The doctrine of the perseverance of the saints is clearly taught in Scripture.

Yet it is often misunderstood and misrepresented, in four different ways in particular. Chapter 17 addresses each of these distortions and presents the truth in its biblical form.

Who will persevere?

Those who question this doctrine sometimes point to people who have made a profession of faith at some point and have continued to live as Christians for some time, but have ultimately fallen away, renounced their profession and shown no interest in the faith for the rest of their lives. How can it be said of such people that they persevered? Clearly they did not. And yet they said that they had, at one point, been converted to Christ.

This objection misunderstands the doctrine, in that it misidentifies the people to whom the doctrine applies. Paragraph 1 of chapter 17 is quite clear on this point: those who persevere to the end satisfy three criteria: they are 'accepted in the beloved' by God, they are 'effectually called and sanctified by his Spirit' and they have been 'given the precious faith of his elect'. In other words, the doctrine concerns true believers, God's elect who have been called to genuine, saving repentance and faith in Christ. This coincides with Jesus' teaching in the verses quoted above, where he is speaking of his 'sheep', whom the Father has given to him, for him to come into this world and redeem (Jn. 10:14–16; 17:6). It is these, and these alone, who will persevere to the end.

What does it mean to persevere?

A second kind of misunderstanding occurs when it is suggested that this doctrine opens the way for believers to live as they please, rather than to be careful to walk in faith and obedience to Christ. The misunderstanding here centres upon what it means to persevere. The promise is not that someone who professes faith in Christ but lives a life of sin will gain eternal life anyway. The truth that is taught here is that the genuine believer will indeed persevere – in a life of faith, repentance, grace and holiness (though not sinless perfection) until the end.

Paragraph 1 of chapter 17 underlines this by stating that 'the gifts and callings of God are without repentance'. It goes on to detail what this means in practice, in the Christian's daily life: God 'still [continually] begets and nourisheth in them faith, repentance, love, joy, hope, and all the graces of the Spirit unto immortality'. These beautiful words derive from the First London Baptist Confession of Faith, 1644 (Article 19), and so do not appear in either the Westminster Confession or the Savoy Declaration. They make clear that the life of the genuine believer is marked to the end by the work of God in the soul, the fruit of the indwelling Holy Spirit.

It is therefore impossible for a believer to live a life of unbridled ungodliness. Even if they should fall into serious sin and backslide for a considerable period of time, they will infallibly be restored to faith and godliness before the end.

This aspect of the doctrine is addressed specifically in paragraph 3 of chapter 17. The Confession here admits the reality that genuine believers may fall into serious sin and that that condition may endure for some while. Peter's threefold denial of Christ is cited as scriptural evidence of this. Such a condition is attributed to three causes: temptation, remaining corruption and neglect of the means of grace.

The serious, adverse spiritual consequences of such a course are also spelled out in the paragraph, with reference to David's experience following his sin with Bathsheba as recorded in Psalm 51. Such people 'incur God's displeasure and grieve his holy Spirit'; they lose their Christian joy and find no pleasure in spiritual things, as they 'come to have their graces and comforts impaired [and] their hearts hardened'; they harm others by their backslidings; and they 'bring temporal judgements upon themselves', maybe in terms of sickness (as in 1 Cor. 11:30) or in other kinds of difficulty, trouble or tragedy coming upon them.

The believer cannot depart from a life of holiness with impunity. Yet for those who are truly the Lord's, as the closing words of chapter 17 assure us, 'they shall renew their repentance and be preserved through faith in Christ Jesus to the end'.

What about the believer's troubles?

A third misunderstanding of this truth relates to the believer's experience. The doctrine of perseverance does not teach that the Christian's life is one of unmixed joy and ease. On the contrary, as paragraph 1 spells out, believers may well experience during the course of the Christian life 'many storms and floods' which shall, however, 'never be able to take them off that foundation and rock which by faith they are fastened upon'.

The 'temptations of Satan', as well as 'unbelief', may for a while cloud or obscure 'the sensible [experiential] sight of the light and love of God', but God is 'still the same' and he will keep them by his power 'unto salvation, where they shall enjoy their purchased possession' for they are 'engraven upon the palm of his hands' and their names are in the book of life 'from all eternity'.

These comforting words, again, come from the 1644 Baptist Confession (Article 23). They express in the most reassuring terms the great truth taught by the Apostle Paul at the end of the eighth chapter of his letter to the Romans, that there is nothing in heaven or on earth that is able to 'separate us from the love of God that is in Christ Jesus our Lord' (Rom. 8:39).

How then do we persevere?

The final misunderstanding of this doctrine attributes the saints' final perseverance to their own will: they continue in faith because they, unlike others, are fully committed by an act of their will to follow Christ despite all adversity. Such a view ascribes the honour for reaching the finishing post to the believer, rather than to the Lord. Paragraph 2 of chapter 17, by contrast, denies that the perseverance of the saints depends 'upon their own free will'. They continue in faith, not because they are better than others at facing down troubles and opposition, but for reasons that are rooted firmly in the nature and work of God himself. This paragraph identifies five grounds, in God, for the 'certainty and infallibility' of the perseverance of the saints.

Firstly, it is founded upon 'the immutability of the decree of election', which itself flows from 'the free and unchangeable love of God the Father'. What could be more certain than the free and loving choice of the creator and sustainer of the universe, the omnipotent, eternal one who is sovereign in all things! This takes us back to the affirmation of paragraph 1 of the chapter, where we saw that the doctrine of perseverance applies to genuine believers, the elect of God, and to them only. It is because they are chosen by the Father, in love, that they persevere. Verses from Romans are cited in support (Rom. 8:30; 9:11, 16; 5:9, 10).

Secondly, their perseverance is founded upon 'the efficacy of the merit and intercession of Jesus Christ and union with him'. Again, what more solid grounds for perseverance could there be, than the finished work of redemption accomplished by the incarnate Christ, with whom the believer is united?

Thirdly, there is mentioned the 'oath of God', an addition of the Savoy Declaration to the equivalent paragraph of the Westminster Confession. Citing the argument in Hebrews 6:17, the paragraph points us to what God has promised he will do, in order to affirm the certainty of the saints' perseverance.

This certainty is further reinforced, fourthly, by 'the abiding of his Spirit, and the seed of God within them' (see 1 Jn. 3:9), underlining how the three persons of the Trinity are each distinctly involved in the work of perseverance.

Finally the 'covenant of grace' supplies a further guarantee that every one of the elect will indeed continue in a state of grace until the end, citing the 'permanent covenant' promised by Jeremiah (Jer. 32:40).

It is these great truths, fixing the believer's perseverance to the end firmly in the nature, purposes and work of the triune God, which inform Augustus Toplady's great hymn, 'A debtor to mercy alone', with its climactic final lines:

Yes, I to the end shall endure,
    as sure as the earnest is given;
more happy, but not more secure,
    the glorified spirits in heaven.

Assurance of grace and salvation (chapter 18)

Assurance is a believer's certain, personal knowledge that he or she is 'in the state of grace, and may rejoice in the hope of the glory of God'. It is another doctrine that is much misunderstood, yet if rightly grasped and experienced provides tremendous comfort to the believer. Chapter 18 opens by setting before the reader two kinds of believer – firstly, 'temporary believers, and other unregenerate' people, and secondly, 'such as truly believe in the Lord Jesus, and love him in sincerity'. Both kinds, according to paragraph 1, may attain to some form of assurance that they are indeed saved: the first assurance is false and amounts only to presumption, while the second form is true and certain.

Who may be assured?

This teaches some important truths and raises some vital questions. It shows that not everyone who claims to be sure that they are a believer is in fact so, as is plain from the Lord's teaching about those who will come to him on the last day saying, 'Lord, Lord', yet who are not his at all (Mt. 7:22–23). We should therefore not be too quick to accept all professions of faith as genuine and we need to be careful to examine ourselves to see whether we 'are in the faith' (2 Cor. 13:5). There is indeed such a thing as temporary faith, as the experience of Simon in Samaria demonstrates (Acts 8:9–24). As paragraph 1 puts it, people 'may vainly deceive themselves with false hopes and carnal presumptions of being in the favour of God and state of salvation, which hope of theirs shall perish'. We must be on our guard against such 'false hopes'.

The fear of presumption must not, however, drive us to think that we can never be certain about the genuineness of our faith. The second half of paragraph 1 teaches the comforting truth that true believers in Christ, 'endeavouring to walk in all good conscience before him', may indeed 'in this life be certainly assured that they are in the state of grace, and may rejoice in the hope of the glory of God, which hope shall never make them ashamed'.

Contrary to the Roman Catholic teaching that such assurance is attained in this life only by a very few, the reformed confessions unanimously instruct us in the biblical teaching that assurance is within the grasp of all true believers. The writings of the Apostle John, in particular, are cited in support: John wrote his first epistle to believers 'that you may know that you have eternal life' (1 Jn. 5:13). It is difficult to give these inspired words any sense other than that genuine assurance of salvation is an experience to which any believer may aspire.

This is backed up in paragraph 1 by the citation of the famous 'we know' verses in that letter (1 Jn. 2:3, 'we know that we know him'; 3:14, ' we know that we have passed from death to life'; 3:19, 'we will know that we belong to the truth'; 3:24, 'we know that he remains in us'). In the light of such statements in God's word, it is impossible to deny that Christians may have true assurance of grace and salvation.

How assured may we be?

Chapter 18 is at pains to make clear that this assurance is real and certain. It is not, as paragraph 2 puts it, 'a bare conjectural and probable persuasion grounded upon a fallible hope'. In other words, it is not a matter of weighing up probabilities and hoping that everything will work out in the end, in the way in which a farmer might hope on the basis of his experience of weather patterns that it will soon rain. The assurance of which the Bible speaks is far more certain than that. It is, according to paragraph 2, an 'infallible assurance of faith'.

This is a very strong expression, is it not? 'Infallible' means incapable of misleading – certainly correct. Is this really what the Scriptures promise? The Bible verses cited in paragraph 2 do indeed teach this, speaking of the 'full assurance of your hope' (Heb. 6:11), a hope that is 'an anchor for the soul, firm and secure' (Heb. 6:19), the need to 'confirm your calling and election' so that you 'never stumble' (2 Pet. 1:10) and the witness that the Spirit gives to the believer that 'we are God's children' (Rom. 8:16). Believers may come to a place where they are rightly entitled to believe without doubt that they are truly children of God.

How is this assurance obtained and nurtured?

How then does the Christian come to possess such assurance? For this, we need to ask what this assurance is founded upon. The answer given in paragraph 2 is threefold. Firstly, this assurance of faith is 'founded on the blood and righteousness of Christ revealed in the gospel'. The equivalent passage in the Westminster Confession makes reference here instead to 'the divine truth of the promises of salvation'. The wording of the 1689 Confession places the emphasis on the saving work of Christ – the blood of Christ that cleanses from all sin and his perfect righteousness that is imputed to believers, thereby justifying them completely and forever before a holy and righteous God. As we meditate on the sufficiency of this work of Christ, we grow in confidence that our salvation is certain and so come into greater assurance of faith.

The second element underpinning assurance is 'the inward evidence of those graces of the Spirit unto which promises are made'. In other words, as the believer engages in self-examination and finds in themselves evidence of the fruit of the Holy Spirit as expounded by Paul (Gal. 5:22–23), or the graces listed by Peter in his second letter (2 Pet. 1:5–8), there is a growing sense of the genuineness of their faith and so growth in assurance of salvation.

The third element mentioned in paragraph 2 is seen by many as the pinnacle of assurance and that which truly renders it infallible in the experience of the believer: this is 'the testimony of the Spirit of adoption, witnessing with our spirits that we are the children of God' (see Rom. 8:15, 16). Some would see this as a sense of certainty about one's salvation given by the Holy Spirit directly to the believer. Others would understand it as the work of the Spirit confirming the truths of the gospel in the believer's mind and heart and applying those truths to their conscience so as to confirm that they are truly a child of God. Perhaps it is best to think of these various elements working together, by God's grace, to produce in the believer who perseveres in faith and godliness the 'infallible assurance of faith' of which chapter 18 speaks.

Many genuine Christians struggle with this. For some, assurance is an elevated status attained only by the very few, usually after years and years of patient waiting and yearning. On this view, many believers die without any true assurance of faith. For some at the other end of the spectrum, assurance is of the essence of saving faith and so no one can really claim to be a believer if they do not also have assurance.

The Confession takes neither of these positions. It affirms, in paragraph 3, that a true believer 'may wait long and conflict with many difficulties before he be partaker of it'. One may be genuinely saved yet lack assurance. At the same time, paragraph 3 goes on to encourage the believer to assurance, 'enabled by the Spirit' and 'in the right use of means'.

Assurance, then, is something that the believer may seek, with genuine hope of attaining it. There is in fact a duty on each believer to seek such assurance earnestly, with 'all diligence' (see 2 Pet. 1:10). The fruits of such assurance motivate that quest, as it brings 'peace and joy in the Holy Spirit', 'love and thankfulness to God' and 'strength and cheerfulness in the duties of obedience'.

Can assurance be lost?

The final paragraph of chapter 18 deals with the distressing state of the believer whose assurance is 'shaken, diminished, and intermitted' in various ways. The causes of such negative experiences include negligence on the believer's part in preserving assurance; falling into some special sin that wounds the conscience and grieves the Holy Spirit; 'some sudden or vehement temptation'; or by God's withdrawing from the believer a sense of his favour, the 'light of his countenance', allowing him to 'walk in darkness and to have no light'.

Christians who undergo the last-mentioned affliction, in particular, can feel blindsided by the experience, wondering why they have lost their joy in Christ and perplexed as to how they should react. Paragraph 4 gives hope that assurance will be revived, for the 'seed of God, and life of faith' remain in the believer, even in such extremities. They still love Christ, even if for a while they do not feel his love for them; they love Christ's people; they have a 'sincerity of heart and conscience of duty' still. It is from these abiding realities that God will, in his goodness, eventually restore assurance and by which 'in the mean time they are preserved from utter despair'.

Conclusion

The doctrines of the perseverance of the saints and of assurance are most valuable scriptural truths that are too little known by believers. A recovery of a biblical understanding of these teachings and of an experiential familiarity with them in the lives of God's people would go a long way towards the revival of the church in our day. Let us study these chapters of the Confession in the light of the Bible's instruction in these matters. And let us meditate on these things and so grow in faith, in love for Christ and in the joy of our salvation, to the glory of the triune God and the extension of his kingdom upon earth.

Rejoice, believer, in the Lord,
    who makes your cause his own!
The hope that's built upon His Word
    can ne'er be overthrown.

John Newton

Study questions

1. How does the doctrine of the perseverance of the saints motivate the Christian to live a godly life?

2. What help does chapter 18 give to someone who lacks assurance of salvation?

3. What do these chapters tell you about the experience of living the Christian life?

Further reading

John Benton, *Evangelistic Calvinism: Why the Doctrines of Grace are Good News* (Banner of Truth, 2006)

John Owen, *Christians Are Forever! The Doctrine of the Saints' Perseverance Explained and Confirmed* (abridged, Christian Focus, 2019)

J. C. Ryle, *Assurance: How to Know You Are a Christian* (repr. Christian Focus, 2021)

Thomas Brooks, *Heaven on Earth: A Treatise on Christian Assurance* (repr. Banner of Truth, 2022)

Joel Beeke, *The Quest for Full Assurance* (Banner of Truth, 1999)

Chapters 19 – 21:
Law, Gospel & Liberty

Chapters 19, 20 and 21 of the 1689 Confession deal with topics which believers can have many questions about – the law, the gospel and Christian freedom. What place, if any, does God's law have in the Christian life? Has the gospel not set the believer free from the law? But then does that mean we have no obligations towards God at all? And what does it mean to be free, as a Christian? Free from what and for what purpose?

These are vitally important questions. We need to understand what the Bible teaches about these topics and how they relate to one another. Failure in this area leads Christians into a legalism that burdens their conscience or, at the other extreme, an antinomianism (that is, a rejection of God's law as the rule of the believer's life) that risks throwing off all constraints and embracing an ungodly licence. This in turn harms the precious gifts of Christian assurance, peace and joy, as well as our witness in the world and the reputation of the church, bringing dishonour on the name of Christ.

The 1689 Confession, chapters 19 to 21, are clear and concise in their biblical expression of these vital topics. If we grasp their teaching in these areas, we will be helped enormously in our Christian living to serve the Lord with confidence and joy.

The law (chapter 19)

The chapter begins with the words, 'God gave to Adam a law', reminding us that God is our creator (chapter 4) and so has the right and authority to command us how we are to live.

The law given to Adam

Paragraph 1 tells us about the law that God gave to Adam in Eden, which was of two kinds. Adam received 'a law of universal obedience', which was 'written in his heart'. He knew this law intuitively. He did not need it to be written down for him, for he was inwardly conscious of what it commanded him. He was also given a 'particular precept', which was the command not to eat of the tree of the knowledge of good and evil. This was spelled out to him by God (Gen. 2:16–17), together with the warning of what would happen to him if he broke it (he would die).

This law, says the paragraph, bound Adam 'and all his posterity'. Adam was the federal head of all humanity, our covenant representative before God. Our destiny was bound up with his in the garden of Eden. The law he received required 'personal, entire, exact and perpetual obedience'. No exceptions or excuses were allowed. When Adam disobeyed the law, he brought upon us all the penalty that God had threatened for its breach (see the Confession's chapter 6).

The law that was written on Adam's heart, we are told in paragraph 2, 'continued to be a perfect rule of righteousness after the fall' and formed the substance of the Ten Commandments 'delivered by God upon Mount Sinai'. So here we have a law applicable to all humanity at all times. This is what is called the 'moral law' and is dealt with more fully in paragraph 5, below.

Ceremonial laws

Alongside the Ten Commandments given by God to Moses at Sinai, the Lord gave to the people of Israel other laws and commands. These included what paragraph 3 calls 'ceremonial laws', concerning the worship of God – the sacrifices and offerings that they were to give, the priests who were to officiate, the tabernacle and its furniture in which worship was to take place – as well as laws about food, the treatment of the dead, dealing with certain diseases and other matters of daily life.

All these ceremonial laws were temporary, applying 'only to the time of reformation', that is the coming of Christ. As the 'true Messiah and only lawgiver', Christ had power from the Father to bring these laws to an end; and so he did. They no longer apply, either to the people of Israel or to anyone else. Their purpose was in 'prefiguring Christ, his graces, actions, sufferings, and benefits' and, that having been achieved with the coming of Christ, they were of no further use and so have been 'abrogated and taken away'.

Judicial laws

Other laws were given to Israel, which paragraph 4 calls 'judicial'. These too were temporary; they 'expired together with the state of that people'. In other words, once the people of Israel ceased to be a nation (effectively, following the sack of Jerusalem by the Romans in AD 70) the laws that governed their functioning as a people necessarily also ceased.

The Confession does not spell out what these laws were, but we could think, for example, of the laws about the seventh year and the jubilee (Lev. 25). These make little sense once Israel no longer functioned as a nation and so are not applicable any more.

They are not totally insignificant, however, as 'their general equity' is still 'of moral use'. There are principles of justice and fairness which underlie these judicial laws that continue to be of relevance. Paragraph 4 gives one example, that of the command (Deut. 25:4) that an ox is not to be muzzled while it is put to work treading out the grain. Paul applies the general principle of fairness that lies at the root of this specific command to show the Corinthian believers that those who give their time to gospel ministry should be recompensed for their work (1 Cor. 9:8–11).

The moral law

Are there, then, any laws that God has given to all people for all time? Chapter 19 answers positively: the law that God gave and wrote upon Adam's heart 'bound him, and all his posterity' (paragraph 1, above). It continues, according to paragraph 2, 'to be a perfect rule of righteousness after the fall' and was given by God at Sinai in the form of the Ten Commandments, 'the four first containing our duty towards God, and the other six our duty to man'.

This, says paragraph 3, is called the 'moral' law, it does (paragraph 5) 'for ever bind all'. Here, then, is a law from God which applies to every human being, whenever and wherever he or she lives. It is universally applicable. The obligation to worship the one, true God, the prohibition of murder, theft and adultery and all the other requirements encapsulated in the Ten Commandments bind everyone.

These commands were not introduced at Sinai but have always applied since the creation of man, though they were not codified in writing until given to Moses at Sinai. And they continue in full effect (subject to the change of sabbath day – see chapter 22), despite the dispersal of the people of Israel as a theocratic nation. Paragraph 5 makes clear that Christ in no way reduced or removed the moral law, but if anything strengthened it. In the Sermon on the Mount, Jesus refers to the Ten Commandments and makes clear that they apply, not only to our actions, but also to the inward workings of our minds and hearts. Merely looking at a woman lustfully contravenes the seventh command; simple hatred breaks the sixth.

Paragraph 6 then shows how the moral law applies to the Christian believer. That law does not apply to believers 'as a covenant of works' – it does not condemn, or indeed justify, them. That is because (as chapter 11 shows) the believer is justified by the imputation of the righteousness of Jesus Christ alone, to which the believer cannot and may not seek to add any supposed righteousness of their own under the moral law. Equally, the condemnation of the moral law for the believer's sins has fallen entirely and finally upon Christ on the cross and so is not in any way borne by the believer. It is vital for the believer to grasp these tremendous truths.

This does not mean, however, that the moral law is of no relevance at all to the believer. Quite the contrary, as paragraph 6 makes clear: the moral law is 'of great use to them'. Four benefits are given.

The law, first of all, informs the believer of the will of God and so of their duty under the law. Christians often seek God's will in a rather mystical manner, expecting some special revelation of a detailed plan for the next stage of their life. The Confession, more biblically, directs us to God's moral law as that which directs us as to God's will for us. It is our duty to follow such direction. 'Duty' is not a term much in use among evangelicals today, but it used to be a common way for Christians to speak about their life: is a particular course or decision about my life part of my duty to God, according to his word? We would do well to ask that question more than we perhaps do.

Then the moral law, secondly, shows us 'the sinful pollutions' of our 'natures, hearts and lives', bringing us under further conviction of sin, causing us to humble ourselves for our sin and giving us a greater hatred for that sin, as well as a clearer view of our need of Christ.

Thirdly, the moral law restrains the regenerate in their 'corruptions', as we see how God forbids sin and the things that he threatens for it underline how serious it is. We learn, then, that we may expect 'afflictions' from God's hand as a result, though as chastisement and not as strict punishment.

Finally, we see from the promises attached to the law in God's word how he approves of obedience 'and what blessings' we 'may expect upon the performance thereof', even though such blessings are not earned as something that is due to us, as if under a covenant of works, but come to us by God's grace.

So we see that all these various ways in which the moral law continues to be of use to the believer are perfectly consistent with the gospel – they 'do sweetly comply with it' (paragraph 7). The

Holy Spirit subdues and enables our wills 'freely and cheerfully' to do that which God's law requires us to do.

The gospel (chapter 20)

This chapter, on the gospel and the extent of its grace, was new in the Congregationalist's Savoy Declaration, not being included in the Westminster Confession of Faith. The precise reasons for its inclusion are unclear, but the Congregationalists felt the need for a chapter on the gospel, after that on the law, which brought together various significant truths (mostly expressed elsewhere in these confessions) concerning the gospel of Christ. It was taken up by the Baptists in the 1689 Confession with just a few minor changes.

Law and the gospel

At the outset, chapter 20 makes clear the relationship between the law of God and the gospel: now that the covenant of works is broken (by Adam, in Eden), the only way to eternal life is by the gospel of God's grace in Christ, not via the law. It is by the 'promise of Christ' that God's elect are called and brought to faith and repentance; it is by the gospel that sinners are converted and saved (paragraph 1).

Revelation of the gospel

How do we come to hear this gospel? Paragraph 2 makes clear that we do not learn the gospel from 'the works of creation or providence, with the light of nature'. Christ and God's grace in him cannot be discovered from these sources. It is only revealed to humanity in God's word. It is only through that word that people can come to saving faith and repentance. The preaching of the gospel is essential to the growth of Christ's kingdom on earth.

God's providence in the preaching of the gospel

Why is it that some nations know a great deal more of the gospel than others? Why are there, comparatively, so many gospel churches in the United Kingdom and in North America and so few in, for example, Saudi Arabia? The answer of paragraph 3 is that this is due entirely to God's providence. No 'improvement of men's natural abilities, by virtue of common light received' can affect this. Humanity cannot increase its chances of understanding the good news of Christ by making good use of the natural understanding that we may have from our knowledge of the world or of ourselves, nor by any attempt we may make to live a moral life.

It is God alone who decides where and when the gospel will be preached in the world. This explains the 'great variety' in the extent to which the good news is known in different parts of the globe.

The work of the Holy Spirit

The mere external preaching of the gospel is not in itself sufficient for conversion (paragraph 4). It is only when there is present in this work the power of the Holy Spirit in the regeneration of sinners so as to give them 'new spiritual life' that conversions occur.

Each of these truths can be found elsewhere in the Westminster, Savoy and 1689 Confessions, yet it is helpful to have them brought together in this way, to remind us that it is only by the word of God and the Spirit of God that the gospel reaches the human heart and that the gospel of God's grace spreads to different people and nations, 'merely of the sovereign will and good pleasure of God' (paragraph 3).

Christian freedom (chapter 21)

Christian liberty, or freedom, is one of the forgotten doctrines of contemporary evangelicalism – and the loss is a great one. A true, biblical doctrine of Christian freedom is a tremendous help to the believer's assurance of his or her faith, giving joy in serving the Lord and a conscience that is not constantly plagued by feelings of guilt. Christian freedom was one of the great scriptural truths recovered at the reformation.

Chapter 21 first sets out a wonderful list of the things from which the Christian believer has been freed by the gospel: the guilt of sin and the wrath of God, as well as the 'rigour and curse of the law'; the terrible trio of the world, the flesh and the devil to which every believer was captive before coming to faith in Christ; the 'evil of afflictions' (though not necessarily from afflictions themselves); and the fear and sting of death (though, again, not death itself), the victory of the grave and everlasting damnation.

Positively, paragraph 1 says that Christians have liberty in 'their free access to God' and in the fact that they obey God 'not out of a slavish fear, but a child-like love and willing mind'. This last is a great blessing and indicates the spirit in which we are to seek to obey the Lord. The paragraph adds that Old Testament believers enjoyed these freedoms too, in measure, but New Testament believers are privileged with greater freedom, especially as the ceremonial law does not apply to them and they have 'greater boldness of access to the throne of grace' and 'fuller communications of the free Spirit of God'.

The believer can too easily allow the conscience to be wrongly bound, so that feelings of guilt arise when they should not and the believer feels constrained to act in ways that the Lord does not require. This can be a great burden and flows from a failure to grasp this doctrine of Christian freedom as it applies to the conscience. The chapter states in paragraph 2 the vital principle that 'God alone is Lord of the conscience'. In other words, the Lord alone has the authority to give commands that bind our consciences: he has 'left it [the conscience] free from the doctrines and commandments of men' where these are contrary to, or not contained in, God's word.

This is what the Lord Jesus Christ attacked, for example, in the teaching of the Pharisees, when they treated their traditions as if they were divine commands. We are therefore not to believe doctrines or obey commands out of conscience that are not found in the Scriptures. To fall prey to such things is legalism, which 'is to betray true liberty of conscience'.

Moreover, we must be on our guard against those who may require of us 'implicit faith', which is where they tell us to follow them blindly without a proper understanding of what they teach or why they teach it: they want 'absolute and blind obedience', which is the mark of a cult. We are to refuse to submit to any such requirement. We are to fear God, not man. It is in areas such as these that many believers go astray, wrongly bind up their consciences and so lose joy and assurance of faith.

The chapter ends with a warning and a promise. The warning is against a wrong use of Christian freedom, to 'practise any sin, or cherish any sinful lust'. This is to 'pervert the main design of the grace of the gospel to their own destruction', with the result that they 'wholly destroy the end of Christian liberty'. This is to be carefully avoided. Rather, we are to pursue a true outworking of Christian freedom, liberated by the gospel from the power of sin so as to become 'enslaved to righteousness' (Rom. 6:17–18). This is the aim of Christian liberty, that, as the closing words of the chapter put it, quoting Luke 1:74–75, 'being delivered out of the hands of all our enemies we might serve the Lord without fear in holiness and righteousness before him, all the days of our life.'

Conclusion

Everyone wants freedom, but few know either what it is or where to find it. These three chapters of the 1689 Confession, addressing the law, the gospel and Christian liberty, provide a masterly overview of this vital subject of Christian living. They demonstrate that, in the end, only the Christian faith gives true freedom.

The collect for peace in the order for morning service in the Church of England's Book of Common Prayer addresses the God 'whose service is perfect freedom'. This ancient phrase sums up in a few words the teaching that we have considered from these chapters of the Confession. The Christian believer, standing firm upon the free grace of God in the gospel of Jesus Christ and directed (but not condemned) by God's law, lives a life of true freedom in the service of the Lord.

O that the Lord would guide my ways
    to keep His statutes still!
O that my God would grant me grace
    to know and do His will!

O send Your Spirit down to write
    Your law upon my heart;
nor let my tongue indulge deceit,
    nor act the liar's part.

Isaac Watts

Study questions

1. How do you answer those who argue that the Christian believer is not subject to the law of God in any sense?

2. What does chapter 20 on the gospel mean for the church's mandate to evangelise?

3. Discuss possible threats to Christian liberty in evangelicalism today, for example legalism or an overly authoritarian approach to church leadership.

Further reading

Andrew Bonar, *Gospel Basics: Trusting, Following and Winning Christ* (repr. Banner of Truth, 2011)

Ian Hamilton, *The Gospel-Shaped Life* (Banner of Truth, 2017)

Jonathan Bayes, *The Threefold Division of the Law* (Christian Institute, 2005)

Samuel Bolton, *The True Grounds of Christian Freedom* (repr. Banner of Truth, 1964)

Chapters 22 & 23:
Worship

The worship of almighty God should be the highlight of the believer's life. The gathering of the local congregation week by week on the Lord's Day is to fill the Christian with delight. King David was glad when they said to him, 'Let's go to the house of the LORD' (Ps. 122:1). The reformers and the puritans fought for a worship that was biblical and so properly glorifying to God, to take the place of the unbiblical worship that had been fostered by centuries of Roman Catholic dominance.

The principles for which they battled long and hard are summarised in the Westminster Confession of Faith, chapter 21, 'Of Religious Worship, and Of the Sabbath Day'. For the Baptists, chapter 22 of the 1689 Confession repeats the principles found in the Presbyterian document, with just a small number of changes of wording.

The worship of God (chapter 22)

At its start, chapter 22 asserts that worship is a duty owed to God by everyone. It is by 'the light of nature' that God is known as Lord and Sovereign and as just and 'good unto all'. For that reason, he is to be 'feared, loved, praised, called upon, trusted in and served, with all the heart and all the soul and with all the might' by all.

There is a sense in which, as some strongly assert, the worship of God encompasses all of life (Rom. 12:1). We are to recognise our entire dependence upon him in all we do. We are God's creatures and we owe everything to him – literally. And so we are to give him all that we have – heart, soul and might – and this is our worship. Yet there is a most important and distinct sense in which we worship God when we come to him, individually or with others, specifically to honour him as God and direct to him our praise, worship and adoration. It is this worship which this chapter especially addresses.

The rule of worship

We may not worship God just as we please, as paragraph 1 of chapter 22 makes clear. There is an 'acceptable way of worshipping the true God', which implies that there are unacceptable ways of going about that vital task. This may be news to some believers, who appear to think that it is up to us to decide how we will worship God. No, says the Confession, citing the key verse in Deuteronomy where, in the context of instruction about worship, the Lord says to his people, 'Be careful to do everything I command you; do not add anything to it or take anything away from it' (Deut. 12:32).

So the Confession states, it is God himself who has instituted the acceptable way for us to worship him. It is 'limited by his own revealed will', so that he is not to be worshipped 'according to the imaginations and devices of men, or the suggestions of Satan, under any visible representations, or any other way, not prescribed in the holy Scriptures', citing the second commandment.

That last phrase, 'not prescribed in the holy Scriptures', goes to the heart of a vital distinction that needs to be grasped at this point. All evangelicals are agreed that we should look to the Bible when it comes to determining how to worship God. Some, however, argue that we are free to do anything in worship that is not prohibited by Scripture. Historically, that has been the position of Lutheranism and was taken up by many in the Church of England.

Those who trace their theological pedigree to the reformers, in contrast, hold that we should do in worship only what God has commanded us to do. That is a far more stringent rule, but flows clearly from Scriptures such as Deuteronomy 12:32, cited above, as well as the experiences of Nadab and Abihu, who took it upon themselves to offer to God fire that he had not authorised (Lev. 10) and Uzzah, who died when he touched the ark of the covenant to steady it in its journey to Jerusalem under King David (2 Sam. 6). This accords too with what one would expect – that it is for God to tell us how he wishes us to worship him, not for us to decide how we are going to go about that awesome and fearful task.

Contrary to what many think, this 'regulative principle', as it is known, liberates. We are clear as to what we are to do in the worship of God and how we should go about it. In corporate worship, we are not subjected to merely human ideas about how to worship God, but can be confident that what we are being asked to do as we worship is in line with what God requires. We look then to the word of God to discover how we should worship the Lord. The remainder of chapter 22 of the Confession seeks to summarise the teaching of Scripture on this question.

Whom do we worship?

The second paragraph makes clear that worship is to be addressed to the triune God alone – Father, Son and Holy Spirit – and not to angels, nor to saints; not to Mary, nor to any other person or creature of any kind. It is good to remember the triune nature of the God whom we worship. Our prayers and praise should not be addressed to a generalised 'God' without in some manner recognising that he is Father, Son and Spirit: plentiful references to this should be made in our prayers and songs. Paragraph 2 also makes clear that sinners, because of their sin, can no longer come to God directly in their own name; they must come to him through a mediator – and Jesus Christ is the only mediator (Jn. 14:6; 1 Tim. 2:5).

What are we to do in worship?

Paragraphs 3 to 5 tell us that the elements that are to make up our worship are prayer (Ps. 65:2; 95:1–7), the reading of the Scriptures (1 Tim. 4:13), preaching (2 Tim. 4:2), hearing the word of God, singing (Col. 3:16) and the administration of the ordinances. This forms an exhaustive list of what we are to do together when we meet to worship God.

Prayer and thanksgiving are, as a matter of 'natural worship', required of all people. This refutes those who hold that a command to pray applies only to believers, on the grounds that only believers are heard by God. Paragraph 3 goes on to make that very point – prayer, to be accepted, has to be made in the name of the Son, by the help of the Spirit and according to Christ's will. Only believers can do that. Nevertheless, it remains that everyone ought to pray. Duty is not defined by ability.

The paragraph also informs us of the spirit in which prayer is to be made: 'with understanding, reverence, humility, fervency, faith, love and perseverance' and, if with others, in a 'known tongue'. This is a helpful checklist for our prayer life; if we pray in this manner, we will be saved from a mechanical praying by rote and will be stirred up truly to seek the Lord when we come to him in prayer.

The next paragraph tells us what we are to pray for: for 'all things lawful' and 'for all sorts of men living', but not for the dead, nor for those whom we know have committed the sin unto death – this last category is no doubt included because of the express prohibition in 1 John 5:16, to which the paragraph refers without seeking to define how we may know such a thing. Paragraph 5 makes clear that, on 'special occasions', there should be 'solemn humiliation with fastings', as well as thanksgiving, done 'in an holy and religious manner'. This would cover such events as a national day of prayer or of thanksgiving.

Where are we to worship?

Under the Mosaic covenant, the people of Israel were not to gather for worship just anywhere they pleased. They were to go up to Jerusalem for that purpose (Deut. 12:4–7; see Jn. 4:20–21). Paragraph 6 makes clear that such restrictions no longer apply – we may offer worship anywhere. The restriction that applies under the new covenant is that it be offered 'in Spirit and in truth' (Jn. 4:24).

This should be done daily in families, privately in secret and 'more solemnly in public assemblies' which we are not to neglect

(Heb. 10:25). Church or cathedral buildings are not more holy places than the chapel or the home, or indeed the outdoors. All creation is the Lord's and it is fitting to worship him wherever we are.

When should we worship?

The final two paragraphs of chapter 22 set out the historic puritan doctrine of the sabbath. Under the Old Testament, from creation onwards, the sabbath to be observed as holy to the Lord was the seventh day of the week. That has now changed, since the resurrection of Christ, and under the new covenant it is the first day of the week which is to be observed, in commemoration of that glorious resurrection. This continues until Christ's return.

While there is no express command in Scripture altering the day to the first day of the week, the change may easily be inferred from the practice of the New Testament churches, clearly endorsed by the apostles, as shown in three passages: 1 Corinthians 16:1, 2, where Paul refers to the first day of the week as the day on which the churches were to set aside funds for the collection for the saints; Acts 20:7, which relates how the church at Troas gathered on the first day of the week to hear Paul; and Revelation 1:10, where the Apostle John refers to the 'Lord's Day' as the day on which he was 'in the Spirit' and saw the risen and glorified Christ. Evangelicals today would do well to ponder these verses carefully, in the light of the fact that God at creation (not only at Sinai) laid down the pattern of one day in seven that is holy.

How are we to keep the sabbath holy?

Paragraph 8 gives us three principles to observe. Firstly, there is work to do in advance of the day, by way of preparation. We are to prepare our hearts for worship and we are to order our 'common affairs', so as to be in a position to make the most of the coming Lord's Day. Secondly, on the day itself, we are to 'observe an holy rest all the day'. This means that we do not indulge in our own 'works, words and thoughts' about our 'worldly employment and recreations'. The things that occupied us during the rest of the week – work, daily domestic duties, social life and leisure activities – are to be put to one side.

The aim of this is, thirdly, that we may give the whole of the sabbath day to 'the public and private exercises' of worship and the 'duties of necessity and mercy'. No doubt meals have to be prepared and dishes washed, even on the Lord's Day, and it is legitimate and right to carry out such necessary duties. It is right, too, that we visit those in especial need, of various kinds, or carry out other works of mercy (Is. 58:6–7). Nurses and doctors, policemen and soldiers are still needed, as they are every day, and must be able to work when required.

Yet every effort should be made, so far as practicable, to set the whole day aside especially for the Lord. This is not to be viewed as an unwelcome obligation or drudgery, but as a privilege – so that we may indeed 'call the Sabbath a delight' (Is. 58:13).

Oaths and vows (chapter 23)

This chapter of the Confession may come as rather a surprise to the twenty-first century evangelical. It deals with oaths and vows as 'a part of religious worship'. This is how they were viewed historically, by reformers and puritans.

An oath is an affirmation of the truth of a statement, made in the name of God; a vow is a promise to God. In that sense, both may be regarded as a part of the worship of God. The inclusion of chapter 23 of the 1689 Confession dealing with these topics reflects similar provisions in the Westminster Confession and the Savoy Declaration. In part, this addressed the view held by some that Christians should never use oaths or vows, a view based on Jesus' statement in the sermon on the mount (Mt. 5:34–37).

While Jesus' statement looks superficially like an absolute prohibition of the use of oaths, a deeper consideration of what he says in the light of the whole of Scripture shows that to be an overly literal conclusion to draw. The Lord's concern was with the way in which the people of his day multiplied oaths in petty matters, swearing by all kinds of things (Mt. 23:16–22). In contrast, there are plenty of Old Testament examples of believers swearing an oath in God's name (e.g. Abraham's servant, Gen. 24:3; Elijah, 1 Kgs. 17:1). Examples of oaths and vows can, moreover, be found in the New Testament, whether by the Apostle Paul (2 Cor. 1:23; 2 Tim. 4:1–2; Acts 18:18) or indeed in relation to the Lord Jesus himself, who did not reject the oath by which the high priest called on him to make his confession (Mt. 26:63).

Chapter 23 makes clear, however, that oaths are to be taken only in the name of God and that his name is to be used 'with all holy fear and reverence'. God's name is not to be misused or abused – this is 'sinful and to be abhorred'. The contemporary, thoughtless habit of constantly taking the name of God or of Christ in vain is a grave sin.

An oath may therefore be made, in matters of appropriate weight and seriousness, to confirm the truth of a statement, or when required by lawful authority. An oath of allegiance or an oath in court to tell the whole truth, then, should be taken by believers with due solemnity, considering carefully what they are doing. Where they swear to the truth of a statement, they are to make sure that they indeed know the statement to be true, 'for that by rash, false, and vain oaths the Lord is provoked, and for them this land mourns'.

An oath is to be understood and taken in the 'plain, and common sense of the words; without equivocation, or mental reservation' (paragraph 4). In other words, mind games are not to be used when taking an oath. There is no room in this matter for giving words a meaning which may not have been intended, or which would be regarded as unusual or a distortion of the oath. Nor should someone take an oath while in their own mind they do not in fact consent to or agree with it.

Finally, vows are to be made to God alone (paragraph 5) and, as with oaths, should be made only with 'all religious care and faithfulness'. Not all vows are acceptable: 'Popish monastical vows' of chastity, poverty and obedience are superstitious and sinful and no believer 'may entangle himself' in them. At the time of the reformation, many monks and nuns left their monasteries and convents and married, in contravention of their supposed vow of chastity. The reformers made clear that such vows were unbiblical and so not binding. Although the Roman Catholic Church reproached them severely for this practice, it is clear that such promises are contrary to the word of God and should not be kept.

Conclusion

The framers of the great confessions of faith of the seventeenth century were serious about the worship of God. They were all too well aware of the distortion of biblical worship from which their predecessors had emerged in the Reformation. They themselves had to continue the battle for biblical worship in their own day, against the continuing threat of a resurgent Romanism. Even the liturgy of the Protestant Church of England was not, in the view of many of them, fully reformed in line with God's word and required further work. Many of them suffered for their stand on this issue and some fled to other shores, particularly to New England, because of the persecution that they endured.

The Baptists of that time set out in these chapters of the Confession their settled view on the teaching of Scripture on this vital topic. We have our battles about worship, in our day. Let us give attention to the teaching of our forefathers in the faith and seek to follow in their footsteps in our worship of the holy, triune God.

Glory be to God the Father,
  glory be to God the Son,
glory be to God the Spirit,
  great Jehovah, Three in One:
  glory, glory,
  while eternal ages run!

Horatius Bonar

Study questions

1. Discuss the distinction between the whole-of-life worship that Paul requires in Romans 12:1–2 and the particular worship of God dealt with in chapter 22 of the 1689 Confession.

2. What direction does chapter 22 give us for the various things we should (and should not) do in our meetings for worship?

3. Would you take an oath in court?

Further reading

Terry L. Johnson, *The Christian Sabbath* (Banner of Truth, 2021)

Joseph A. Pipa, Jr., ed., *The Worship of God: Reformed Concepts of Biblical Worship* (Christian Focus, 2005)

Chapters 24 & 25:
Civil Government

Baptists can be expected to be interested in questions of civil government – especially the relationship between church and the state – given the suffering that they have undergone at the hands of the state from time to time. In England, the modern Baptist movement was born in persecution, emerging in the sixteenth and early seventeenth centuries at a time when it was illegal to worship except according to the liturgy of the Church of England. Baptists were imprisoned, fined and exiled and were not free to meet for worship until the Toleration Act of 1689. Baptists across the Atlantic in New England often suffered in a similar manner.

In our own day, state restrictions on what churches in the West may do and say threaten once more. During the Covid pandemic, churches in Britain were ordered not to meet for some months and were then allowed to gather only on strict conditions. The British government is currently considering legislation to ban 'conversion therapy', which could impose significant restrictions on what may be taught in and by churches and what Christians may do (for example, pray), in relation to gender and sexuality issues. Stories appear frequently in the Christian media about the arrest of street preachers, as well as about firms disciplining Christian employees for various expressions of their faith. The relationship of church and state remains a pressing issue in Britain and in other western nations today.

Any difficulties that we might face in the western world, however, pale into insignificance compared with the serious persecution experienced by brothers and sisters in other nations. In Myanmar, where the army is in control, church buildings have been attacked and believers have been driven from their homes and killed. When the Taliban took control in Afghanistan in 2021, they went door-to-door with lists of Christians who have as a result suffered violence and sometimes death. In North Korea, the Bible is an illegal book and its possession can result in many years of harsh imprisonment. In Russian-occupied Ukraine, there are stories of pastors kidnapped and tortured and churches disrupted and closed down. In all these countries – and more – the state interferes oppressively in the life of the church and seeks either to regulate it very closely or to extinguish it altogether.

The church's relationship with the state is, then, a vital matter for Christians to consider carefully. The Bible has a great deal to say on the subject. Chapter 24 of the 1689 Confession addresses the question directly. Chapter 25 then deals with a subsidiary, but related and important question: that of marriage.

Church and state (chapter 24)

The relationship of the church to the state is one of the principal areas in which there have been important differences between Baptists and their Presbyterian and Congregationalist brethren. The different views of each group are reflected in their respective confessions of faith at this point. Presbyterians tend to see the strongest connection between church and state, Baptists the loosest, with Congregationalists somewhere in between. Despite these important differences, significant agreement also exists between the three groupings on these vital matters.

Government ordained by God (paragraph 1)

Firstly, government is ordained by God as Lord of all. The Confession does not endorse any particular form of government – democracy, monarchy, oligarchy, etc. Its statements are of general application to all. Paragraph 1 of chapter 24 reflects the teaching of the Apostle Paul in chapter 13 of his letter to the Romans, stating that 'God the supreme Lord and King of all the world, hath ordained civil magistrates'. The reference to the 'magistrate' is the word commonly used in seventeenth-century confessions of faith to speak of anyone holding public office, from the monarch to his ministers of state down to the lower ranks of local government. These rulers, governors and officers hold office by the authority of God himself. As Paul himself put it, 'There is no authority except from God, and the authorities that exist are instituted by God' (Rom. 13:1). For those of us who live in a democracy, we must remember that those whom we elect to political office ultimately gain their authority, not from the voters, but from God.

Paul probably wrote his letter to the Romans when Nero was emperor. The Baptists put together the Second London Confession in 1677, when Charles II was on the throne. It is an understatement to say that neither Nero nor Charles favoured true Christian believers – under Nero, they were put to death in horrible ways, while under Charles those who dissented from participation in the national church were harried, imprisoned and fined. Yet those same Christians, in each case, urged that their rulers must be viewed as holding their authority from God. This is true, whatever the political affiliation of our government and however much we may disagree with what they are doing.

The paragraph goes on to set out the scope of the magistrate's authority, the purposes for which it is to be used and the means that God has supplied for the achievement of those purposes. The magistrate is 'under [God] and over the people'. The magistrate is not without responsibility. Charles I had claimed that kings, by divine right, could do whatever they saw fit. The Confession denies this. The magistrate is answerable to God himself yet has authority over the people whom they govern. The people are therefore to obey the magistrate's rule (within the limits laid down in paragraph 3 – see below).

The objectives for which the magistrate's authority is to be exercised are the glory of God and the good of the people – so not, by implication, to indulge the magistrate's own whims and pleasures. This underlines that public office is a high calling, requiring selflessness and a well-developed sense of responsibility. For the achievement of these ends, the magistrate has 'the power of the sword' – words reflecting Romans 13:4. It is legitimate for the authorities to use force to achieve the objectives of their office.

These include, positively, the 'defence and encouragement of them that do good' as well, negatively, as 'the punishment of evildoers', language that again closely reflects Paul's teaching in Romans 13:3–4.

The Confession thus allows the governing authorities a wide degree of discretion in the discharge of their responsibilities. The whole scheme of the criminal law – police forces to detect crime and arrest suspects, courts to try cases and sentence offenders, prisons, fines and other penalties to punish and to deter evil – is a legitimate and necessary use of the magistrate's authority. Equally, the magistrate is to use his powers to encourage the good – this could include schemes to relieve poverty, to improve employment and social conditions and to meet health and educational needs.

It is not possible to interpret either the Confession or the teaching of the New Testament in a manner that mandates a particular political stance or validates one political party over another. These are issues on which sincere, godly believers will differ. At the same time, it is noteworthy that the Confession, reflecting Paul's teaching in Romans 13, uses moral categories to delimit the magistrate's responsibilities – it is 'them that do good' who are to be defended and encouraged, while 'evildoers' are liable to 'punishment'.

Christians in politics (paragraph 2)

Baptists agree with Presbyterians and Congregationalists, secondly, on the lawfulness of Christians holding political office. This is the subject of paragraph 2: 'It is lawful for Christians to accept, and execute the office of a magistrate, when called thereunto.' Some evangelicals believe that Christians should never become involved in politics: Christians belong to Christ's kingdom which is not of this world. While there are no doubt many challenges to the Christian who chooses to go into politics, the Confession, in line with reformed thinking generally, does not oppose it in principle.

It does, however, state that those who hold public office must exercise that office 'especially to maintain justice and peace' in a manner consistent with the laws of the land. Christian rulers may even, for such purposes, 'wage war upon just and necessary occasions'. So there is no inherent contradiction in a Christian holding public office and exercising civil authority in an earthly kingdom. They do not thereby negate their Christian witness or their allegiance to Christ's heavenly kingdom, provided that they discharge their office consistently with the principles that the Confession sets out in its summary of biblical teaching.

Christian duties towards authorities (paragraph 3)

The third area in which the various denominations agree in this area relates to the duties of Christian believers with regard to those who govern them. These are set out in paragraph 3, which is based on chapter 48 of the First London Baptist Confession of 1644. Although its wording therefore differs from that of the equivalent provisions of the Westminster Confession and the Savoy Declaration, the substance of the three statements is the same. Christians are to obey the authorities set over them and they are to pray for them.

Christians are to submit to the authorities. We should pay our taxes, observe rules and regulations and obey the lawful instructions of those who are set over us in the land. We should do this willingly, whole-heartedly and without complaining. This obedience, however, has limits: it is required 'in all lawful things

... in the Lord'. There is no obligation to obey the authorities when they try to command something that is in fact unlawful. Christians are permitted to make use of the laws of the land to challenge the lawfulness of orders or decisions of civil authorities. And the believer may not obey the authorities where to do so would cause him to disobey Christ. Within those limitations, we should obey, 'not only for wrath but for conscience sake' – in other words, not only for fear of the consequences of disobedience but to keep our consciences clear of offence.

The command to pray for those who rule over us is taken from Paul's instructions in 1 Timothy 2:1–2. It covers all who are in authority, at whatever level. Its aim is that the church may be able to live holy lives and witness for Christ peaceably, without disturbance from hostile individuals or groups, or from the state itself. Although we accept that persecution is a part of living a godly life, as Paul states in his later letter to Timothy (2 Tim. 3:12), it is legitimate and right to hope and to pray that we would be left free by the state to live 'a quiet and peaceable life, in all godliness and honesty', as this third paragraph puts it. This is not so much for the sake of our own ease and comfort, as for the progress of the gospel and the glory of God (1 Tim. 2:3–7).

Spheres of church and state power

The major difference between the 1689 Confession and the presbyterian and congregationalist confessions lies in what is left out of the 1689 document. Both those other documents have statements which give to the civil authorities more or less responsibility for the upholding of true religion. The stronger statement is in the Westminster Confession, chapter 23 paragraph

3 of which gives the civil magistrate the authority and duty 'to take order' for the preservation of peace and unity in the church, for maintaining divine truth 'pure and entire', for the suppression of blasphemies and heresies, for the prevention or reformation of corruptions and abuses in worship and discipline and for the due settlement, administration and observing of all ordinances. For these purposes, the magistrate may call and attend synods and 'provide that whatsoever is transacted in them, be according to the mind of God'.

The Savoy Declaration, chapter 24 paragraph 3, is rather milder, obliging the magistrate 'to encourage, promote, and protect the professor and profession of the Gospel' and discharge his duties 'in a due subserviency to the interest of Christ in the world'. This would involve the suppression of blasphemy and errors that go to the root of the Christian faith, but not to interfere in other matters over which sincere believers may disagree.

The omission of any such statement in the 1689 Confession reflects the early realisation by Baptists that, under the New Testament, church and state are to be separate: each has its own sphere of operation and one is not to encroach upon the other. Questions of doctrine and church practice are for the church to regulate, not the state. Just as the church is not to tell the government how to run the economy or defend its territory, so the civil authorities have no right to dictate to the church how to organise its meetings or what to teach. It is interesting to note that American Presbyterianism revised chapter 23 of the Westminster Confession in 1788 to bring it much more into line with the principle of the separation of church and state.

Marriage (chapter 25)

There are fewer more relevant ethical topics today than marriage. Who can marry whom? How should it be done? What is it for? What level of commitment does it require? All these questions are debated in western society today. Sadly, that society increasingly tends to proffer unbiblical and immoral answers – and, even more sadly, many Christian denominations are following them. In Britain today, at the time of writing, the Church of Scotland permits same-sex marriage ceremonies and other denominations have taken or are considering moves in the same direction. In this context, the teaching of the 1689 Confession on marriage, reflecting as it does the historic, biblical teaching of the worldwide church on the matter, is of vital importance.

The Confession, in agreement with the Westminster Confession and the Savoy Declaration, defines marriage as being 'between one man and one woman' (paragraph 1). A man may not 'at the same time' be married to more than one wife, nor a woman to more than one husband. So bigamy is forbidden, but widows and widowers are free to marry. The Confession does not define what a man or a woman is. That would have been totally unnecessary in the seventeenth century. The idea that one's sex may differ from one's gender, or that a man may become a woman or vice versa, would have been incomprehensible then (as it was to most people until very recently).

Three purposes for marriage are given in paragraph 2: the 'mutual help of husband and wife', the 'increase of mankind with a legitimate issue' and 'for preventing uncleanness'. The statement changes the equivalent part of Westminster and Savoy by omitting their reference to 'the increase ... of the Church with an holy seed'. It is logical for those who hold to infant baptism, with its belief that baptised infants are in some sense members of the church, to hold that marriage between Christian parents may serve, simply through the act of procreation, to increase the church. Baptists could never subscribe to such a position. Although we consider our children to be privileged – and for that reason may even be called 'holy', as Paul does in 1 Corinthians 7:14 – in that they grow up in a home run on Christian principles, going to church regularly and hearing the gospel from their earliest days, we see no biblical basis for saying that they are members of the church, unless and until they themselves come to saving faith in Jesus Christ and are then baptised.

Finally, in paragraphs 3 and 4, the Confession deals with the question of who may marry whom. It begins with a broad statement: 'It is lawful for all sorts of people to marry, who are able with judgement to give their consent'. This lays down the vital principle of informed consent as foundational for marriage. No one can be forced into a marriage, nor is marriage possible for those who lack the capacity to give consent. Subject to that, however, there are no restrictions on who may marry. Marriages between individuals of different backgrounds, colour, language or ethnicity are entirely acceptable, provided that there is consent on both sides. This is an important affirmation.

For the Christian believer, however, the position is restricted. Christians are to 'marry in the Lord' (paragraph 3) and so true believers are not to marry 'Infidels or Idolaters', nor 'such as are wicked in their life, or maintain damnable heresy'. Marriage to unbelievers, those who live ungodly lives or those who deny essential truths of the Christian faith is inadmissible for believers. Finally, there are restrictions on marriage between those who are closely related. The Bible lays down rules on this subject, in Leviticus 18, to which the Confession (paragraph 4) makes reference. These rules are to be observed, says the Confession, whatever the relevant law of the land states. Incestuous relationships can never be lawful.

The 1689 Confession, like the congregationalist Savoy Declaration, entirely omits the paragraph in the Westminster Confession dealing with the subject of divorce. The reasons for this are unclear. It was not because the Baptists completely prohibited divorce or viewed it always as unbiblical. It may have been that, like the Congregationalists, they thought that there was insufficient agreement among them on the matter and so it was not a suitable topic for a confession of faith. In any case, at that time, divorce was available only to the very rich and influential and so the matter would have had little application to Baptists.

Conclusion

The teaching of the Confession on the church's relationship with the state and on marriage remains of great relevance today. Baptists need to understand clearly the Bible's teaching on these vital matters. These chapters of the Confession supply concise, accurate instruction which reflects scriptural doctrine as understood by Baptists. We would do well to study and think carefully about the implications of this teaching for our witness in society today, that the name of Christ may be honoured in the manner in which we seek to live out its principles among the communities to which we belong.

O Lord our God, arise!
    the cause of truth maintain,
and wide o'er all the peopled world
    extend her blessèd reign.

               Ralph Wardlaw

Study questions

1. How do you pray for those in authority in the nation and for Christians in politics?

2. What difference does the biblical teaching on the authority of the state make to the Christian's daily life?

3. Discuss the issues raised by current challenges to a biblical understanding of marriage, for the nation and for the church.

Further reading

Oliver Allmand-Smith, *Under God, Over the People: The Calling and Accountability of Civil Government* (Broken Wharfe, 2022)

D. M. Lloyd-Jones, *Christian Marriage* (Banner of Truth, 2012)

Chapters 26 & 27:
The Church

Over recent years, the evangelical world (including the more conservative and reformed part of it) has seen very sad cases of sexual immorality and abuse among certain of its church leaders. This gives us cause to mourn deeply. We must pray for those who have suffered from such sins, that they would find comfort and help from the Lord and from his faithful people. We must not forget to pray for those guilty of conduct that has caused such harm and distress. We cannot adopt a spirit of superiority or triumphalism in such matters, for we are all capable of the same sins; rather, we should examine ourselves and our own practices and seek the Lord in repentance, for grace to persevere in faith and truth.

Why raise this matter in a chapter on the church? Because, I am convinced, a closer attention to the instructions of the New Testament as to the government and life of the local church would help avoid such abuses. This is not only a twenty-first-century concern. In the seventeenth century, Philip Nye and Thomas Goodwin pointed out in their preface to John Cotton's well-known work, *The Keys of the Kingdom* (1644), that abuse of power by church leaders is one of the main reasons why (as Cotton argued in that work) properly ordered churches should form themselves into associations of churches. Proper, biblical order in our churches does not guarantee the absence of abuse, but it does set in place essential safeguards and practices which reduce the opportunity for it.

Independent and Baptist churches have, from the outset, laid great emphasis on this. The True Confession of 1596, composed by Independents who had separated from the Church of England, devotes no fewer than twenty-two paragraphs to the subject of proper church order. This approach is reflected in the 1689 Confession, in which the longest chapter is this chapter 26. The fifteen paragraphs that make up this chapter constitute one of the most faithful, clear and balanced statements of the biblical teaching on the topic of the local church that there is. Careful study of it, put into practice, will go a long way towards protecting the healthy, fruitful life of the local church.

The Church (chapter 26)

What is the church? (paragraphs 1 to 4)

The Confession begins this chapter with a statement about the universal church – that is, the church considered as a single, unified entity made up of all its members from every age and part of the world. This 'catholic or universal church' is made up of 'the whole number of the elect', past, present or future. It includes Old Testament believers as well as all who have been or will be gathered under the new covenant in Christ and so are his. This is the true church, which 'may be called invisible' (as it is defined by 'the internal work of the Spirit and truth of grace'). Christ is her head and she is his 'spouse, the body, the fulness of him that filleth all in all'.

It is vital that the church of Jesus Christ be seen in this world, as a testimony to the gospel and as the means by which that gospel is proclaimed to the peoples of this earth. That is why Christian believers must gather in 'particular congregations' (paragraph 2), or, as we might call them today, local churches.

But who is to belong to such congregations? Here we find an issue on which the Baptists take a different course from both the Presbyterians, in their Westminster Confession of Faith, and the Congregationalists, in their Savoy Declaration. While those denominations admit children of believers as members of their churches, the Baptists do not (whilst holding such children in high regard and admitting the great privileges that they enjoy as the offspring of believers). Nor, in contrast to the established churches of the land, do Baptists admit as members of their churches everyone in the parish who has been baptised, or christened as an infant, and has not repudiated the Christian faith.

For Baptists, then, those who make up the local church satisfy two conditions: they profess the faith of the gospel and live lives that are obedient to God. They must show their sincerity in these matters by not rejecting any of the foundational truths of the gospel and by not living unholy lives. No mention is made here of a requirement for baptism, which on the face of it is surprising. The explanation for this is given in the Appendix to the Confession, which explains that there was insufficient agreement between the framers of the Confession on the precise relationship between baptism and church membership for this issue to be addressed in the document.

So someone who rejects the triune nature of God, or the deity of Christ, or who believes that our works contribute to our salvation, by way of example, should not be admitted to membership of a local church, unless and until their views on these essential matters are brought into line with the clear teaching of Scripture. Similarly, someone in an adulterous or homosexual relationship, or whose life is characterised by drunkenness or swearing, should not become a church member, unless and until there is real repentance and a turning from such sins.

That is why Baptist churches have procedures for admitting new members – the aim should be simply to test the matters outlined above, so far as we are able to do so (for we cannot read one another's thoughts or search each other's hearts). We admit freely that we cannot always be right on these matters. So the Confession (paragraph 3) states that even the 'purest churches under heaven are subject to mixture and error'. Some so-called churches have degenerated so far, either in their teaching or in the lifestyle that they allow among their members, that they can no longer be recognised as true churches of Christ, but are rather 'synagogues of Satan'. Despite this, the Confession asserts that the kingdom of Christ will never die out in this world.

Our Lord Jesus Christ is the head of this church, appointed to that office by God the Father. All power in the church is vested in him. Thus the Pope of Rome cannot be recognised 'in any sense' as the head of the church. In these ecumenical days, when it is fashionable to recognise as Christians any who say that they are, it is deeply unfashionable to dispute the claims of the Pope. Nevertheless, we must do so, for the claim is false.

The Confession (paragraph 4) goes on to say that the Pope is 'that Antichrist, that man of sin, and son of perdition' of whom Scripture speaks. It needs to be understood that this is so by virtue of the papal office, rather than the personal qualities or characteristics of the individual occupying that office. It is the claims which the Roman Catholic Church makes about the papacy that gave rise to this assertion – particularly the claims relating to papal headship over the universal church and the false doctrine that the papacy upholds. Views as to the interpretation of the relevant New Testament passages (2 The. 2:8–9 in particular) vary. Yet it is difficult to contest the fact that the Roman Catholic Church, in its official doctrine, makes assertions about its head, the Pope, which fundamentally conflict with the claims of the Lord Jesus Christ as head of the church.

The formation and ordering of particular churches (paragraphs 5 to 7)

The Lord Jesus as head of the church exercises that authority by calling people to himself, to trust and follow him. He commands these to belong to local churches for their mutual edification and for public worship. It is essential to keep in mind this emphasis. We have a tendency to think of churches as 'our' churches – under 'our' control, run on 'our' principles, as we think fit, and for 'our' ultimate benefit. Such thinking, whether on the part of the pastor, church officers or the congregation generally, is quite wrong and, in the end, destructive of true church life. Christ is the head of the universal church and of the individual congregations of his people that make up that church.

It is Christ, then, who gathers his people into these congregations. He does this 'through the ministry of his word, by his Spirit'. The preaching of the word in the power of the Holy Spirit is the means that Christ has chosen to use for the calling of the elect – 'those that are given unto him by his Father' – out of the world, to 'walk before him in all the ways of obedience, which he prescribeth to them in his word'. It is not, in the end, the cleverness of our strategies, the attractiveness of our meetings or our ability to befriend and get alongside unbelievers, but Christ himself, by his word and Spirit, who adds people to his churches.

Those who are so added become members of their local church and should then live in obedience to Christ in his word – not perfectly and sinlessly, as the Confession has already shown (see chapters 9.4, 11.5, 13.2), yet 'visibly manifesting and evidencing (in and by their profession and walking) such obedience (paragraph 6). They do this in churches, by willing consent walking together, 'giving up themselves, to the Lord and one to another', in submission to Christ's commands. In other words, the church is not a place for us to display our gifts or simply enjoy the worship; it is, rather, the place where we serve one another and together serve Christ.

And for this purpose, each local church has been given, by Christ, all the power and authority that it needs to carry out its work (paragraph 7). It does not need the permission of any other body – whether some higher church body or some arm of the state – in order to carry out that work. It may engage in all the acts of worship and of discipline to which Christ calls each of his churches in his word. While churches should obey the law of the land in matters such as planning regulations, health and safety and safeguarding, they need no permission from anyone as to how, when and where they worship or as to the manner in which they conduct and regulate church life. They have all that they need for such purposes directly from Christ himself.

Church office (paragraphs 8 to 11)

Christ has given instruction as to how churches are to organise themselves in the exercise of the power that he confers on them. Many have disputed this, claiming that the New Testament gives no specific instruction as to the government of local churches and leaves such matters to our own wisdom and discretion. That is not the view of the Confession.

Paragraph 8 affirms that a local church, properly organised 'according to the mind of Christ', consists of officers and members. The officers are to be 'chosen and set apart by' the church duly gathered for that purpose. Church officers are not imposed by some other body, but appointed by the members of the church themselves, in accordance with God's word. The officers so appointed are then to be responsible for the execution of the power of the local church and for the administration of the ordinances (of baptism and the Lord's Supper, dealt with in chapters 28 to 30).

The Confession provides for two offices in the church, according to the teaching of the New Testament: elder and deacon (paragraph 8). It is the Holy Spirit who fits and gifts individuals for such office (paragraph 9). They are to be chosen for office by 'the common suffrage of the church itself', that is, by debate and vote of the membership of the local church. An elder so appointed is to be set apart by the church, by fasting and prayer and the laying on of hands by the existing eldership. Deacons are set apart by prayer and the laying on of hands.

Pastors, who are set apart particularly for the ministry of the word and prayer, are to be shown all due respect for the sake of their work. They are to be financially supported by the congregation, so that they do not have to become 'entangled in secular affairs' and may be able to exercise the ministry of hospitality (paragraph 10). This last point is important and sadly neglected by many churches who do not provide sufficiently for their pastor. While the Confession envisages that the work of preaching will be carried out primarily by pastors, it provides also (paragraph 11) for 'others also gifted and fitted by the Holy Spirit for it' to be approved by the local church to preach. These were known at the time as 'gifted brethren'; the practice of formally recognising such people in this manner deserves to more widely observed, as it provides a proper church control over who is preaching, which is in turn necessary to help preserve the integrity of what is taught in our churches.

Church discipline (paragraphs 12 & 13)

One of the great omissions of any age in the history of the church is a biblical church discipline. This was of concern to the puritans, who lamented the lack of any real discipline in the Church of England in their time. Although the dissenting churches that emerged after the restoration of the monarchy in 1660 tended to take discipline more seriously, its exercise can be fraught with difficulty on every side. It can lead, on the one hand, to abuse of authority, where it is exercised harshly or in inappropriate areas of life; on the other hand, its neglect will lead inevitably to a decline in the standard of church life and the effectiveness of the church's testimony.

The Confession simply makes clear that, firstly, every believer should be a member of a local church. Sadly, this is ignored by many – through ignorance or a misunderstanding of what church membership truly is, or perhaps from previous bad experience, or simply from a desire to retain an unbiblical independence of spirit. Christians should join themselves to a local church and commit themselves in the body of that church to serve Christ and one another, with the other members of it. This gives them access to what the Confession calls the 'privileges of a church' (paragraph 12) and also places them 'under the censures and government thereof, according to the rule of Christ'. We are to be subject to the rule of the elders in the local church (Heb. 13:17).

It is not every aspect of our lives that comes under the discipline of the church. The elders have no right to interfere with how parents bring up their children or how members conduct themselves in their workplace, unless there is some clear breach of biblical instruction that is sufficiently serious to require church action. But where that is the case, such action needs to be taken, for the good of the individual involved, to restore them to a healthy Christian walk with Christ, as well as for the testimony of the church.

The Confession is also realistic about the fact that believers sometimes fall out with one another. The biblical instructions for such a situation are expected to be followed (Mt. 18:15–20). The offended party is then expected (paragraph 13) to leave the matter with the church, for due process to take its course. They should not cease to attend meetings or cause any kind of disturbance to the order of the church in the meantime, but are to 'wait upon Christ, in the further proceeding of the church'. The Confession here demonstrates the practical, biblical realism that is so often required for healthy church life in a fallen world.

Associations of churches (paragraphs 14 & 15)

So far, we have seen the Confession emphasising and working out the principle of the independence of the local church. Yet that is not all that needs to be said. The early Baptist churches were keen to emphasise their unity together in Christ. They accordingly operated regional and national associations of churches which met regularly to discuss matters of mutual concern and to seek the progress of the gospel. This was not regarded as an option, but an obligation: they were independent, but not isolationist. Sadly, today, we tend to be both independent and isolationist. Such a situation requires change – we need to recover our forefathers' emphasis on independent churches working together.

Churches are to 'hold communion' among themselves, 'for their peace, increase of love, and mutual edification' (paragraph 14). At their association meeting they discussed questions of doctrine and practice that arose among them; they sought to give financial help to poorer churches and supply preachers to those that lacked them; and where possible they worked together to further the cause of Christ in areas where there was little or no gospel witness.

Additionally, the Confession (paragraph 15) provides for the settling of disputes in or among churches, by these means. It is made clear that an association of churches has no 'church-power properly so called' or 'any jurisdiction over the churches themselves'. The association may investigate disputes and difficulties among its churches and may report its findings to the churches, but has no power to impose any solution – that is left to the individual church or churches concerned. The Confession thereby preserves a proper biblical balance between the independence of the local church and the need for the churches together to maintain a good testimony among their members and in the world.

Fellowship in the church (chapter 27)

Chapter 27 consists of just two paragraphs. The first sets out the principle that all believers are 'united to Jesus Christ their head, by his Spirit and faith'. We enjoy a wonderful unity together, in Christ. This does not make us 'one person with him' – we each retain our own individuality and personality. Rather, we have fellowship with him 'in his graces, sufferings, death, resurrection and glory'. This is a tremendous truth, which believers would do well to meditate carefully upon, for our encouragement in this sad, fallen world.

Because of our union with Christ, however, we also are 'united to one another in love' and 'have communion in each other's gifts and graces'. This too is wonderful and should be treasured. We do not follow Christ merely as individuals. We do so in company – indeed, in union – with all other believers. We are, consequently, 'obliged to the performance of such duties, public and private, in an orderly way, as do conduce to their mutual good, both in the inward and outward man'. Because we are united one with the other in Christ, we should serve one another, in whatever appropriate ways we can, for one another's good – in material and outward ways, as well as in spiritual and inward ways.

The second paragraph spells this out in more detail. We are to keep up a 'holy fellowship and communion in the worship of God' and in 'other spiritual services' for one another's benefit.

This emphasises the importance of gathering regularly in the local church for worship and for fellowship with one another – this is not to be neglected.

We are also to help one another in 'outward things', to the extent that we are able to do so. This is to be done especially for those who are close to us, either by family connection or in the local church, but not exclusively so – we have an obligation to all who are 'of the household of faith', wherever they may be, so that, 'as God offereth opportunity', we should give help wherever it may be needed and we are in a position to do so. At the same time, the Confession makes clear that we retain ownership of the things that belong to us: we are not communists, but believe in and uphold the right to private property. All this reflects carefully what we read of the life of the early church in Jerusalem, for example, in the opening chapters of the book of Acts.

Conclusion

These two chapters of the 1689 Confession are extraordinarily valuable. Their teaching is greatly needed in our day, when there is much confusion about the place and operation of local churches in the Christian life. We would do well to study these chapters carefully, in the light of Scripture, and seek to implement what they say in our churches.

> I love Your kingdom, Lord,
> the house of Your abode,
> the church our blest Redeemer saved
> with His own precious blood.
>
> Timothy Dwight

Study questions

1. Identify from Scripture the duties and the benefits of belonging to a local church.

2. How is true fellowship best nurtured in a local church?

3. What would be the benefits and the potential risks of belonging to an association of churches?

Further reading

David Skull, Andrew King & Jim Sayers, eds., *Pure Church: Recovering God's Plan for Local Churches* (Grace Publications, 2022)

John S. Hammett, *Biblical Foundations for Baptist Churches: A Contemporary Ecclesiology*, 2nd edn. (Kregel, 2019)

Jeremy Walker, *Providing for Pastors* (EP Books, 2023)

Ryan King & Andrew King, eds., *Association: Local Independent Baptist Churches in Fellowship and Mission* (Grace Publications, 2021)

James M. Renihan, *Edification and Beauty: The Practical Ecclesiology of the English Particular Baptists, 1675-1705* (Wipf & Stock, 2009)

Chapters 28 – 30:
The Ordinances

Few questions of church life have sparked as much controversy as have baptism and the Lord's Supper. At some point fairly early on, the church began to baptise infants and the practice became almost universal for many centuries, until believer's baptism became common again (in the West at least) in the early seventeenth century. At that time, our forefathers in the faith had to fight hard for their conviction that baptism, if conducted biblically, was to be administered, not to infants, but only to those who had made a credible profession of saving faith in Jesus Christ. For this belief, they were mocked and despised by many and attacked in print. On occasion, the attacks were physical – in the early years of the Reformation, some baptists were drowned by the authorities for denying the validity of infant baptism.

The Lord's Supper became corrupted in medieval times by the Roman Catholic doctrine of transubstantiation, which was formalised by the Fourth Lateran Council in 1215. This unbiblical doctrine teaches that the bread and the wine, when consecrated by the priest during the Roman Catholic mass, become the true body and blood of Christ. To the senses – sight, taste, feel, etc. – (the technical name is in their 'accidents'), the bread and wine remain unchanged, but in their 'substance' (which cannot be seen, tasted, felt, etc.), they are changed ('transubstantiated') really and actually into the very body and blood of Christ. During the Reformation, Protestants were burned alive for denying transubstantiation.

Although violence over these questions is rare today, the issues themselves have not been resolved in a manner that satisfies all. Bible-believing Christians today differ not only about who should be baptised, but about the manner in which baptism should be performed: immersion, affusion (pouring) or sprinkling. And Baptists differ among themselves over who precisely should be admitted to the Lord's Supper and on what terms, some preferring a more open table and others a stricter approach. The 1689 Confession remains deliberately neutral on this last question, as those who subscribed it were 'not at a full accord' among them on it, as the Appendix to the Confession states.

It is therefore not surprising to find that chapters 28 to 30 of the 1689 Confession, on the ordinances, differ substantially from the equivalent parts of the Westminster Confession and the Savoy Declaration. Each of the confessions has a chapter that introduces the topic, setting out its view on what baptism and the Lord's Supper are in general terms, before devoting a chapter to each of the ordinances (called 'sacraments' in those other statements of faith).

The ordinances in general (chapter 28)

Chapter 28 of the 1689 Confession is very short, containing just two paragraphs of one sentence each. It makes four affirmations, as follows.

1. Baptism and the Lord's Supper are 'ordinances of positive and sovereign institution'. There are only two such ordinances, in contrast with the seven sacraments of the Roman Catholic Church. The term 'positive' here means that they are specially instituted by direct, express command; if there were no special instruction about them, we would have no way of knowing that we should engage in them. This is important, because it makes clear that we are to derive our practice of these ordinances entirely from the teaching that we have about them in Scripture (apart, of course, from matters of general concern such as the time and place of performing them). They are also said to be of 'sovereign' institution, that is, laid down by one who has authority to do so – they are not the result of negotiation, nor are they optional. These terms underline the importance of observing carefully all that we are taught about these ordinances.

2. It is the 'Lord Jesus the only lawgiver' who has 'appointed' them. They are not ordinances laid down by the church or any particular congregation. They are common to the body of believers in every place and every age. The identification of the 'Lord Jesus' as the one who has appointed them further underlines that these ordinances belong to the new covenant. The Confession does not repeat the language of the Westminster and Savoy documents which teach that

the new covenant ordinances are in spiritual terms 'for substance, the same' as the 'sacraments of the old testament'.

3. The church is to continue to baptise and to share in the Lord's Supper 'to the end of the world', in other words, until Christ's return. The Apostle Paul intimated precisely this in his teaching on the Supper in his first letter to the Corinthians (1 Cor. 11:26). While there is no specific text stating this in relation to baptism, neither is there any time limit placed on the ordinance – the command to baptise continues in force until Jesus returns in glory.

4. Who may baptise and administer the Lord's Supper? This is a controversial question among Baptists. Some argue that any believer may do this; others say that only those properly qualified may do so. The 1689 Confession takes the latter line: only those 'who are qualified and thereunto called according to the commission of Christ' may administer the 'holy appointments' (paragraph 2). It is important to be clear what this means in practice. The Confession does not teach that an ordinance performed by an unqualified person is not a valid ordinance. What the Confession is saying is that the church needs to take care about who carries out the ordinance: a congregation needs to ensure that only qualified persons do so. The question as to who precisely this indicates was discussed by the early calvinistic Baptists, who agreed that it was elders and possibly 'gifted brethren'

(that is, recognised preachers) who should administer the ordinances.[1]

Baptism (chapter 29)

It might be expected that the statements on baptism made in the 1689 Confession would differ entirely from those of the Westminster Confession or the Savoy Declaration. In fact, they are remarkably similar in several respects. It is to the credit of our Baptist forefathers that even here, at the most obvious point of disagreement with their Presbyterian and Congregationalist brethren, they still sought to follow the wording of the older confessions, so far as they could do so in good conscience. The opening statement of the nature and significance of baptism is similar, if not identical, in these various confessions, as are the affirmations about the use of water and the trinitarian formula to be used. There are, however, differences.

As already stated, the Baptists preferred the word 'ordinance' to Westminster's 'sacrament' (as also in chapters 28 and 30 of the Confession), perhaps because the latter word is that used in Roman Catholic teaching on baptism and the Eucharist, though Reformed Baptists have generally been content to use either term. The ordinance of baptism is not so closely tied in the Confession to the local church as is the Lord's Supper, which is specifically to be observed 'in his churches' with ministers presiding. The focus

---

1 See James M. Renihan, *Edification and Beauty: The Practical Ecclesiology of the English Particular Baptists, 1675-1705* (Wipf & Stock, 2009), p. 141.

of the statements on baptism is rather on 'the party baptized', for whom baptism is a 'sign' of four vital things.

The first two of these relate to the believer's union with Christ. Baptism is a sign, firstly, of 'his fellowship with [Christ], in his death, and resurrection', and, secondly, of 'his being engrafted into [Christ]'. Paul's teaching in the opening verses of Romans 6 speaks of how believers have been 'baptised into Christ Jesus'. They have therefore been 'baptised into his death' and 'buried with him by baptism', so that 'just as Christ was raised from the dead by the glory of the Father, so we too may walk in newness of life' (Rom. 6:3, 4). Our union with Christ, which stands at the root of all the blessings which we enjoy in Christ, is impressed upon us in our baptism as we are symbolically lowered into the grave and emerge triumphant in Christ's victory over death.

Then baptism is a sign of 'remission of sins'. In the testimony of his conversion that the Apostle Paul gave to the crowds in Jerusalem after his arrest there, he told of how Ananias had come and instructed him, 'Get up and be baptised, and wash away your sins, calling on his [the Lord's] name' (Acts 22:16).[2] The same connection between washing and the remission of sins can be found in Paul's letter to Titus, where he writes of the 'washing of regeneration' (3:5). The obvious connection between baptism and washing from sin must not be overlooked: it is not, as some believe, that the water of baptism itself literally washes from sin; rather, that washing, which is brought about by faith in the blood of Christ,

---

2 This is probably the correct reference in the 1689 Confession at this point, rather than the one actually printed, Acts 26:16.

is a powerful aspect of the symbolism of baptism which should be allowed to make its full impact on the one being baptised.

Finally, the Confession tells us that baptism is a sign that we now belong to God through Christ, 'to live and walk in newness of life'. Baptism has significance for the whole of the Christian life, not only for its commencement. The union that we have with Christ in his death and resurrection leads to this, argues Paul (Rom. 6:4). This is why the believer cannot continue to live in sin (Rom. 6:2) – the 'old self' has been crucified with Christ and we now enjoy new life in union with the risen Christ. This is how we are to think of ourselves and this is how we are now to live (Rom. 6:6, 11, 12).

Again, baptism reminds us of all this and, as we meditate on the significance of our baptism, should bring home to us with great force the radical nature of the change that has been brought about in us. We have not merely turned over a new leaf, or cast off a few bad habits, or even changed our religion. We are new creatures in Christ, with a new life in union with him. Just as Christ's body lay dead in the tomb and just as we have gone down into the water, so the old way of sin is dead to us and we have risen to an entirely new life in Christ. So let us live!

The remainder of the chapter on baptism is straightforward. The second paragraph answers the question, who should be baptised? The 'only proper subjects' of the ordinance are those 'who do actually profess repentance towards God' and 'faith in, and obedience to, our Lord Jesus'. There is no room for infant baptism – and no space here to enter into the rather more complex arguments used by those who adhere to the Westminster Confession to seek to justify it from the Scriptures. Though we dearly love our paedobaptist brethren in Christ and have a deep respect for their theological learning and heritage as well as their godliness of life, we are not persuaded by their arguments on this point and believe that the 1689 Confession sets out the biblical position: baptism is for believers only.

The final two paragraphs of the chapter confirm that water is to be used in baptism. Baptism is to be expressly trinitarian, 'in the name of the Father and of the Son and of the Holy Spirit', reflecting precisely the instructions of the risen Christ to his disciples in the great commission (Mt. 28:19) – baptism in the name only of Jesus, as practised by some, is not sufficient. Baptism is to be by 'immersion, or dipping of the person in water' (paragraph 4), immersion being 'necessary to the due administration of this ordinance'. The phrase 'due administration' means that, to be done rightly and in an orderly, biblical manner, the person baptised should be immersed in the water. The use of other modes may not entirely invalidate the baptism, but it is immersion that is the proper mode.

The Lord's Supper (chapter 30)

This chapter is significantly longer than that on baptism, no doubt indicative of the larger number of issues that need to be addressed. There are eight paragraphs, each odd-numbered one setting out a positive statement about the Supper and the following, even-numbered one refuting a misunderstanding connected with that statement.

The chapter begins with a statement about the nature of the meal: it is for a 'perpetual remembrance' of Christ's sacrificial death and for a 'showing forth' of it. So far as believers are concerned, the Supper confirms them in their faith and in all its benefits, providing spiritual nourishment and growth in Christ and reinforcing their responsibility to carry out the duties that they owe him. It has a horizontal, as well as a vertical, effect: 'to be a bond and pledge of their communion with him, and with each other'. In contrast, paragraph 2 warns that the meal involves no 'real sacrifice' or offering of Christ of any kind, contrary to Roman Catholic teaching. It is 'only a memorial' of that offering and a 'spiritual oblation of all possible praise unto God' for it.

The next two paragraphs deal with the administration of the ordinance. This, according to the third paragraph, is to be done by ministers, who are to pray and bless the elements, thereby setting them apart 'from a common to an holy use'. They are to 'take and break the bread' and 'take the cup', partake of the elements themselves and give them to those communicating (paragraph 3). The cup is not to be denied to the people, the elements are not to be worshipped or carried about for adoration, and they are not to be reserved for 'any pretended religious use' (paragraph 4). These are or have been all common Roman Catholic practices utterly foreign to the biblical nature of the ordinance and rightly condemned by the Confession.

The Confession, like the Westminster and Savoy documents, then asserts (paragraph 5), in opposition to Roman Catholic understanding, that the bread and wine in the Supper remain bread and wine, 'in substance, and nature ... truly, and only ... as they were before'. Although they may sometimes be called the body and blood of Christ, there is no change of any kind in them. The Roman Catholic doctrine of transubstantiation, for the rejection of which many Protestants died as martyrs, is squarely and explicitly denied (paragraph 6) as 'repugnant to Scripture' as well as to 'common sense and reason' and is superstitious and idolatrous.

The final two paragraphs of the Chapter deal with the reception of the elements in the Lord's Supper. What effect does partaking of them have (paragraph 7)? It is, asserts the Confession, only believers who benefit, by faith. They 'inwardly by faith, really and indeed, yet not carnally, and corporally, but spiritually receive, and feed upon Christ crucified and all the benefits of his death'. This is a very careful statement of the historic reformed position, which (as we have seen) bluntly denies transubstantiation, yet wants to preserve the truth of, for example, 1 Corinthians 10:16, that the cup and the bread that we share in the Supper are indeed a 'sharing' in the blood and body of Christ.

In what sense is this the case? Not in a material or physical sense, but spiritually, says the Confession; and yet, this does not mean merely symbolically, but rather 'really and indeed'. A purely memorialist view of the Supper is thereby rejected, in favour of something far richer and more satisfyingly reflective of the teaching of Scripture on the Supper. The chapter ends with a strong warning (paragraph 8) about the dangers of participation by the 'ignorant and ungodly' – that is, the unconverted and those who are refusing to live a holy life trusting in Christ. These cannot partake of the supper without 'great sin', whereby they become 'guilty of the body and blood of the Lord, eating and drinking judgement to themselves'.

Conclusion

It is impossible to read these chapters of the 1689 Confession without being impressed by the seriousness with which the early Baptists treated the ordinances. Their careful, considered reflection on biblical teaching led them to retain some statements of the Westminster Confession on the topic and to alter others, in some places radically. Baptism and the Lord's Supper are sometimes treated today with a lightness that is unbecoming of those who profess to believe the Bible to be their only authority in faith and life. Thoughtful study of the paragraphs which make up these three chapters will go a long way to restoring a right understanding of and attitude towards these vital parts of a faithful Christian life.

Amidst us our Belovèd stands,
and bids us view His piercèd hands;
points to His wounded feet and side,
blest emblems of the crucified.

What food luxurious loads the board,
when at His table sits the Lord!
The wine how rich, the bread how sweet,
when Jesus deigns the guests to meet!

Charles Haddon Spurgeon

Study questions

1. Think about the biblical truths concerning the believer which baptism expresses. What are the implications of these blessings for the Christian life?

2. How should the believer best prepare to receive the Lord's Supper?

3. What are suitable subjects for meditation and prayer during the Lord's Supper?

Further reading

David Kingdon, *Children of Abraham: A Reformed Baptist View of the Covenants*, revd. edn. (Grace Publications, 2021)

Brian Russell, *Baptism: Sign and Seal* (Grace Publications, 2021)

Michael A. G. Haykin, *Amidst Us Our Beloved Stands: Recovering Sacrament in the Baptist Tradition* (Lexham Press, 2022)

Chapters 31 – 32:
The Last Things

As a young Christian, I was keenly interested in what the Bible had to say about the end of the world. I studied the books of Ezekiel, Daniel and Revelation to try to discern the sequence of events that would lead to Armageddon and the return of Christ. The Lord Jesus' sermon on the Mount of Olives (Mt. 24; Mk. 13; Lk. 17) and Paul's teaching in his letters to the Thessalonians supplied more material for my research. Who was the Antichrist? Would China cross the Euphrates and invade Israel? What is the mark of the beast? Then there was the question of the rapture – would this take place before the 'Great Tribulation', in the middle of that seven-year period (as I thought it to be), or at the return of Christ? And how would the millennium then unfold, precisely?

The final two chapters of the 1689 Confession, dealing with the last things, answer none of these questions – indeed, such topics as these are not even mentioned. At one level, this is not surprising, as dispensational ideas such as the rapture emerged only in the nineteenth century. At the same time, many Christians in the seventeenth century were preoccupied with a fairly literalist understanding of the passages referred to above. Many believed that the return of Christ would usher in a millennial period of great blessing on earth. Especially during the period of political instability of the 1640s and 1650s, some expected the millennium to come about very soon.

All the great confessions of faith that were put together during that period or soon after – the Westminster, Savoy and Second London Baptist Confessions – studiously ignore these questions, which concern only the details of the events that lead up to the end. The clear implication is that Christians should not fall out over such matters and should focus instead on what the Bible clearly teaches.

Chapters 31 and 32 of the 1689 Confession thus concern, firstly, the question of what happens to individuals when their life on this earth comes to an end and then at the resurrection on the last day (sometimes referred to as 'personal eschatology' – 'eschatology' meaning the study of the last things). This is dealt with in chapter 31. Then, secondly, questions related to the nature, purpose and unfolding of the last judgement are addressed, in chapter 32 (sometimes called 'general eschatology').

Personal eschatology (chapter 31)

This chapter answers the question, what happens to me when I die? This important question is plagued by a great deal of confusion – even among Christian believers. Some of God's people today have rather vague ideas of the condition they will be in after the end of their life on earth; some seem to regard their body after death as of little significance. What does chapter 31 tell us about the teaching of the Bible on these vital subjects?

Firstly, the chapter makes clear in its first paragraph that, when a human dies, the soul is separated from the body. In chapter 4 of the Confession, we learned that humans were created 'with reasonable and immortal souls'. At death, body and soul go to different destinations: 'The bodies of men after death return to dust, and see corruption'. God made humanity from the dust of the ground (Gen. 2:7) and, after the fall, it is to dust that our bodies return when we die (Gen. 3:19). Hence the familiar words at a burial service, 'earth to earth, ashes to ashes, dust to dust'.

In contrast, the souls of those who die 'return to God who gave them' – they 'neither die nor sleep'. It was important for the Confession to affirm this: many have believed that, at death, the believer enters into soul-sleep, until the resurrection on the last day. They are perhaps led to this conclusion by the references to believers who have died as 'sleeping' (from which idea we obtain the word 'cemetery', from the Greek word for sleep). What the New Testament conveys by referring to dead believers in that way, however, is that believers' bodies are sleeping until the resurrection – for they have been laid in the ground; in contrast, their souls live on, awaiting that great day. There is no basis in the Bible for teaching that the soul sleeps. After death, the soul remains very much alive and conscious. But what does the soul of a dead person experience?

Chapter 31 answers this question in two parts. All souls 'return to God who gave them', but God's manner of dealing with them varies tremendously. The 'souls of the righteous' are 'then made perfect in holiness' and 'received into paradise where they are with Christ and behold the face of God, in light and glory; waiting for the full redemption of their bodies'. Each of these phrases fills the believer with great joy. (The Confession's reference here to the 'righteous' means those who are righteous in Christ, justified by faith in him). The soul of the believer will immediately be brought to a condition of perfect holiness, in paradise, with Christ, beholding God's face.

In this 'intermediate' state, we lack bodies and we await full vindication and the consummation of all things at the last day. This is not the very best condition, therefore, which is still to come – hence we will be 'waiting' for 'full redemption'. Yet it will be a glorious condition, full of joy (Ps. 16:11), peace and love in the presence of God. No wonder that Paul wrote that 'to die is gain' and 'far better' even than serving Christ in this life (Phil. 1:21, 23). These words comfort us in the face of the uncertainties of death and what lies beyond – something that no one now living has ever experienced and so can tell us nothing about. If the apostle looked forward to it with such great anticipation, so may we.

It is a very different story, however, for the soul of the unbeliever after death. It too returns to God, but for a very different end. For 'the souls of the wicked are cast into hell'. This is, again, not the final state of the ungodly, but a temporary condition, 'where they remain in torment and utter darkness, reserved to the judgement of the great day'. There is no possibility of moving from one of these conditions to the other, as the Lord Jesus made clear in the story of the rich man and Lazarus (Lk. 16:26). There is no hope of any kind of a second chance after death. Nor does the soul of the unbeliever at death enter a state of suspended animation, or some kind of neutral zone while the day of judgement is awaited. It does not enter purgatory (for which there is no biblical basis). As Jesus' story shows, unbelieving souls will be 'in torment' and 'agony' (Lk. 16:23, 24).

What then happens to these – believing and unbelieving souls – at the return of Christ on the last day? And what about those who are alive at that time? This last question is answered in paragraph 2 in relation to Christians: they 'shall not sleep but be changed'. That is, they will not die at all. The paragraph goes on, with regard to believers and unbelievers, to say that 'all the dead shall be raised up'. So there is a general resurrection of all who have ever lived, at the end of the age and the return of Christ. The Confession is silent as to the precise fate of unbelievers alive at that point – maybe it assumes that they die under the wrath of the Lamb (Rev. 6:16–17) and are immediately raised again.

Paragraph 2 is specific about the bodies with which the dead are raised – they are 'the self same bodies and none other' that they had in life. This underlines the importance of our bodies, even when dead. It is those bodies that are raised – we do not receive completely new bodies at the resurrection. For this reason, Christians are well advised to prefer burial to cremation and, in any event, proper respect should always be shown to the human body even when dead. But our resurrected bodies are not unchanged: they will have 'different qualities', as Paul teaches in 1 Corinthians 15:42–49. These changed bodies are then 'united again to their souls for ever'. We will once again be embodied souls, as we are now, but with bodies as well as souls that are immortal.

And of course there is a distinction here, again, between the resurrected state of the believer and that of the unbeliever, as paragraph 3 teaches. The resurrection of the unbeliever – the 'unjust' – is 'by the power of Christ' (and not, as for the believer, in life-giving union with Christ), for Christ is God and it is by him that all are raised; but it is 'to dishonour'. The details of what this means, such as we know them, are given in the following chapter, but here it is simply made plain that, for the unbeliever, the resurrection at the last day will be a most terrible experience. The single word 'dishonour' expresses all the horror of hell that the Bible teaches and which is summarised in chapter 32.

For the believer, by contrast, the resurrection of the body is 'by his [Christ's] Spirit' – the difference in wording perhaps reflecting simply that in the general resurrection it is the power of the triune God that is at work – and is 'unto honour'. This is the precise opposite of the state of the resurrected unbeliever. The word 'honour' implies all the wonderful things that the Bible teaches about the final state of the Christian, again as will be summarised in chapter 32. This is underlined by the final words of the paragraph, that our bodies will 'be made conformable to his [Christ's] own glorious body'. Like Christ, we will inherit bodies that are incorruptible, glorious and without fault or weakness, disability or possibility of illness. We shall have, as Paul puts it, a 'spiritual body' (1 Cor. 15:44), that is, a body utterly under the control of and filled with the Holy Spirit.

The last judgement (chapter 32)

If chapter 31 looks at what happens to us individually after death, chapter 32 tells us about the last judgement in more detail. It makes plain, in paragraph 1, that God is in complete control of this day. It is he who has 'appointed' it and so it will take place when he decrees. He will be the judge and, as he is righteous, so it will be a judgement 'in righteousness'. As Paul preached in Athens, this judgement will be 'by Jesus Christ' (Acts 17:31), to whom the Father has given 'all power and judgement'.

Who will be judged on that day? The 'apostate angels', that is all devils and demons along with Satan himself, and 'all persons that have lived upon the earth' – an all-inclusive description covering every human being there has ever been or will be. Animals will not be judged on that day, for they do not have a rational soul, but all humans will be called to account. This judgement will be most extensive, as it will require an account of 'thoughts, words, and deeds'. No aspect of life will be neglected; all will be thoroughly considered. And the outcome is that each will 'receive according to what they have done in the body, whether good or evil'.

This will have radically different outcomes for the elect from that for unbelievers, as paragraph 2 makes plain. The outcome for the elect is 'eternal salvation', 'everlasting life', 'fulness of joy and glory' and 'everlasting rewards, in the presence of the Lord'. There need be no fear for the believer that all their sins will be paraded before the human race on that great day, for these are all covered and paid for in full by our great high priest, Jesus Christ, through that one great sacrifice of himself for all time (Heb. 9:28). The Bible teaches that there will be rewards for faithful gospel service and loss for some, though not loss of salvation itself (1 Cor. 3:12–15). This should spur the believer to persevere in faith, love and obedience in this life (Heb. 6:10).

For the unbeliever, it is again very different. They will be sentenced to 'eternal damnation' as 'reprobate ... wicked and disobedient', to be 'cast into eternal torments, and punished with everlasting destruction from the presence of the Lord and from the glory of his power'. This is not annihilation, as some have wanted to argue, but a state of conscious punishment, in body and soul, which is, terribly, without end. By these means, paragraph 2 teaches, God shows both 'the glory of his mercy' and 'his justice' (Rom. 9:22–23).

When will all this take place? As Jesus said, we do not know and are not told (Mt. 24:36). As paragraph 3 states, however, we are taught that this day is actually coming – and we need to be 'certainly persuaded' of this – for two purposes: as a deterrent from sin and 'for the great consolation of the godly, in their adversity'. As Christians suffer in this life for their faith, they can take comfort in the knowledge that a day is coming when all wrongs will be put right and justice will triumph over wickedness. At the same time, paragraph 3 teaches that we are deliberately not told when the day will arrive, so that we 'shake off all carnal security, and be always watchful' – for if we knew the date, we might be tempted to indulge in sin, neglecting the Lord and his commands, until the time came closer. Instead, we should, as the Confession exhorts us in its closing words, 'ever be prepared to say, *Come Lord Jesus, Come quickly, Amen*'.

A word on the Appendix

Although that brings to an end the Confession itself, in its thirty-two chapters, an additional document was appended to the original edition published in 1677 and to the 1688 printing, although not to later ones. Of contemporary modernised editions, the Appendix appears in that produced by Jeremy Walker and published as *Rooted and Grounded*. The purpose of this document was to explain why its framers held to the doctrine of baptism taught in chapter

29 of the Confession, particularly that baptism was only for those 'who do actually profess repentance towards God [and] faith in, and obedience to, our Lord Jesus', and why they would therefore not baptise infants. Before they give their reasons for this, however, they make the following important introductory points.

1. The 1689 Confession is deliberately designed to demonstrate that, in the 'fundamental articles of Christianity', Baptists are in agreement with 'all other true Christians'.

2. The Confession sets out what they 'hold and practise', so that there is no need for doubt about this matter.

3. They hold their paedobaptist brethren in high regard, despite their differences, and have no desire to be alienated from them but would rather, as opportunity presents itself, share in their labours and maintain peace, each holding to their own principles as they understand them.

4. They are willing to be shown that they are wrong and will take seriously any effort, 'in the spirit of meekness', to demonstrate this.

With that introduction, the Appendix embarks on a substantial defence of the baptist position. After politely distancing themselves from those (particularly in the Church of England) who require adult sponsors to express repentance and faith on behalf of infants being baptised, the framers of the document argue that the bestowal of a covenant sign must be performed in the manner explicitly laid down in Scripture. This was the case for circumcision in the Old Testament, which was not applied to all who were in the covenant (in particular, females). Thus 'it depends purely upon the will of the lawgiver, to determine what shall be the sign of the covenant, unto whom, at what season, and upon what terms, it shall be affixed'. The seal of the new covenant, they argue, is the 'indwelling of the Spirit of God'. They cite the words of the theologian John Lightfoot, who had been a member of the Westminster Assembly, to the effect that circumcision was given to Abraham as 'a seal of the righteousness of faith which in time to come the uncircumcision (or the Gentiles) should have and obtain'; Lightfoot goes on, as quoted in the Appendix: 'Abraham had a twofold seed, natural, of the Jews; and faithful, of the believing Gentiles'. No express inference is drawn from these words, but the implied argument is clear: the covenant sign is now to be given only to believers.

The Appendix then deals with various passages of Scripture commonly used to argue for the baptising of infants. Without detailing the precise points made in each case, these are: Paul's statement about the holiness of the children of one believing parent (1 Cor. 7:12); passages of Scripture describing the baptism of whole families; Jesus blessing the children; Peter's statement in Acts 2:39 that the 'promise is for you and for your children'; and the commands addressed to children in the epistles. In each case, arguments are given in response, designed to show that these passages are not inconsistent with believers' baptism.

The Appendix closes with further exhortations to love and unity among brethren who may differ in these and other matters not deemed fundamental to the faith. One specific question mentioned concerns differences among Baptists – that some hold to churches being formed only of baptised believers (i.e. those baptised on profession of faith) and others 'have a greater liberty' – in other words, would admit to church membership (and so, it must be assumed, to the Lord's Supper) believers who were baptised as infants. The Confession is thus deliberately neutral on this point.

And so, where there are differences among believers that 'are not of the essence of Christianity', but there is agreement 'in the fundamental doctrines thereof', the framers of the Confession and Appendix believe 'there is sufficient ground to lay aside all bitterness and prejudice, and in the spirit of love and meekness to embrace and own each other therein; leaving each other at liberty to perform such other services (wherein we cannot concur), apart unto God, according to the best of our understanding'.

We would do well, in our day, to take heed of such worthy and Christ-honouring sentiments.

The sands of time are sinking;
    the dawn of heaven breaks;
the summer morn I've sighed for,
    the fair, sweet morn, awakes:
dark, dark hath been the midnight,
    but day-spring is at hand,
and glory, glory dwelleth
    in Immanuel's land.

Anne Ross Cousin

Study questions

1. Consider the enormous implications of the day of judgement. How does this affect our daily life in this age?

2. What things are left behind when we die and enter the 'intermediate state' (before Christ's return) and what things are still to be accomplished?

3. How much do you contemplate the return of Christ? How can you think more about it?

Further reading

William Hendriksen, *The Bible and the Life Hereafter* (Baker, 1959)

Edward Donnelly, *Heaven and Hell: What Comes after Death?* (Banner of Truth, 2001)

Iain H. Murray, *The Puritan Hope: A Study in Revival and the Interpretation of Prophecy* (Banner of Truth, 1971)

Grace Publications seeks to serve Christ Jesus and his church by producing biblically faithful books that bring the truth of the gospel home to us. Our titles range across church health, Baptist history and doctrine, and Christian living.

Please visit our website to view our full catalogue and to access free articles and media designed to help you grow in your faith.

www.gracepublications.co.uk